The Forgotten London League and Cups

Wartime football in London 1940-1942

Jack Rollin

A *SoccerData* Publication

Published in Great Britain by Tony Brown
4 Adrian Close, Toton, Nottingham NG9 6FL
Telephone 0115 973 6086
E-mail soccer@innotts.co.uk
www.soccerdata.com

First published 2016

Cover design by Bob Budd. Background photograph © Popperfoto.

AUTHOR'S ACKNOWLEDGEMENTS

*Much of the ground work for wartime team line-ups was dug out some 30 years ago by the
late Don Aldridge and his notes on the subject provided an excellent starting point for the
in-depth searches that had to be made through the fog of wartime football. The author
would also like to thank Tony Brown for making it into a usable entity plus Glenda Rollin
and Harry Meeson for some valuable technical tweaking!*

Printed and bound by 4Edge, Hockley, Essex
www.4edge.co.uk

ISBN: 978-1-911376-03-3

FOREWORD

The allowance for wartime conditions produced headaches for those bodies trying to keep some form of competitive football alive, but the Football League's decision to radically alter the structure for determining League positions in 1940-41 with goal average replacing the traditional points system proved unpopular with the public. Moreover the unwieldy north and south leagues unwittingly sowed the seeds of a London football rebellion.

Well before the completion of the 1939-40 fixtures the Football League was already drawing up plans for the new campaign. Largely due to the "Phoney War" period that had not interrupted domestic sport to any significant degree, a *status quo* mood had prevailed.

Suddenly it all changed. The German invasion of Belgium and Holland, failure of the Norwegian campaign leading to Winston Churchill coming off the bench to replace Prime Minister Neville Chamberlain then the cancellation of the Bank Holiday, dramatically altered the situation. In the space of a few weeks the bulk of the BEF was forced to evacuate with remnants of other Allied Forces through the little ships miracle of Dunkirk following France's collapse.

Belgian and Dutch refugees were being housed at the Wembley Sports Arena and some Dunkirk survivors were admitted to heart-warming cheers from the 42,399 War Cup Final evening kick-off crowd at the Empire Stadium on 8 June between West Ham and Blackburn. Clearly a re-think for 1940-41 was a priority, especially as a German invasion was still more than a possibility. With the RAF actively taking on the Luftwaffe the outcome of the Battle of Britain was now crucial to the country's survival but the League still put forward several ideas for a new look. These included four regional leagues, a reversion to amateur status as in the Great War and allowance for Sunday play. Then at the AGM on 29 July final decisions were taken. The amateur idea was defeated 26-13 and the other ideas scrapped. Two regional leagues would operate. That night Dover was bombed.

The North Regional League had 36 teams agreeing to participate while the South Regional League had two fewer. Naturally not all teams were expected to play each other twice within a designated region and there remained 18 Football League clubs unable to compete at all for varying wartime reasons, though two came back for the second half of the season and two others then dropped out at the half way stage.

The kick-off was on 31 August with 66 of the 88 Football League teams playing. Neither Chesterfield nor Crewe was in action on the first day. Southend having been designated as a restricted area, United had moved lock, stock and barrel to Chelmsford and its New Writtle Street ground. Anyway Southend's Greyhound Stadium had been taken over by the military. The evacuees had attractive first time visitors in the form of Arsenal who leading by seven clear goals in the first half relaxed and let Southend have a goal. Despite the presence of Ted Drake in the Gunners line-up who scored twice, Leslie Compton usually a deputy defender for Eddie Hapgood went nap with a handful of his own. The crowd was 1,500. Games at Burnley, Liverpool and Newcastle had the better returns estimated at 5,000.

There were nine goals recorded at Selhurst Park with Crystal Palace doubling Chelsea's treble despite England international Vic Woodley being between the sticks for the Pensioners. Luton kicked-off in the evening against Northampton and won 7-1, the start to allow war workers to attend. Overall 80,000 had been the country's estimated aggregate attendance.

A week on and it was a vastly different scenario. The sirens wailed early that sunny 7 September afternoon for what was to be the beginning of Adolf Hitler's third phase of hopefully bringing Britain to its knees, the bombing of London itself. At the Recreation Ground, Aldershot who were leading at half-time 2-1, had added two more goals when the match against Southampton was abandoned. West Ham were losing 4-1 to Tottenham at Upton Park when a halt was called after 70 minutes and Chelsea entertaining Brentford was also ended nine minutes later. However matches at Arsenal, Charlton and Crystal Palace played on for the full 90 minutes.

Between September 1940 and July 1941 there were to be between 45,000 to 50,000 bombs dropped not including incendiaries inflicting heavy casualties on the population. For 57 consecutive nights spanning 7 September to 2 November the raiders visited the Metropolis. Amazingly during this period the London clubs were already planning their own football revolution! Unhappy about fixture arrangements with the calendar due to end in December leaving just the League War Cup to fill the second half of the season, plans were being formulated. One of the prime movers behind the scheme was George Allison manager of Arsenal.

The London FA whose long-serving Secretary was Tom Kirkup agreed to those London clubs wishing to enter the London Combination which was to oversee what was to be a London Cup competition. The same organization had provided the Great War's similar regional fare. Stanley Rous at the Football Association was also involved and since effectively a County FA as in the case of London was responsible, the Football League could have had no legitimate objection to the new tournament. But they kept no record of it.

If there were to be an even number of teams some recruiting was needed to be implemented with only ten effective clubs remaining. Charlton Athletic had decided to quit football for the rest of the season by Christmas, their announcement having been made in November. On 14 December it was stated that after a secret ballot Aldershot and Reading had been elected. Presumably neither Luton nor Watford had made the cut as the nearest of those who had applied. It must have been interesting news for Aldershot beaten 10-1 that day at Norwich!

The designated dozen were split into A and B groups, though while the six in each were nicely split into East and West London, the additional out-of-London teams were deprived of derby games as clearly the voting had been for one vacancy in each group. Since the Football League was not involved in the new competition, its own War Cup that had proved so popular in 1939-40 took precedence in the fixtures giving the London Cup organizers the task of fitting in where possible. It eventually led to a rebellion by the London area clubs that had far reaching consequences for their membership of the Football League.

Given the absence of normal reporting coverage of matches, team changes for spectators relying on two people carrying a blackboard round the ground and with upwards of ten or so alterations not always noted or even filtered through to the correct source for onward distribution, precision towards discovering correct data often assumed archaeologist proportions.

Players were often listed for one team in a club's official programme while actually turning out somewhere else as the relevant changes were not effected. Teams selected, type set and printed on a Friday were often mistakenly set in stone. Pressure on space in truncated newspapers meant scant reference to any sport let alone football reporting. It was a tricky time attempting such accuracy.

THE REBELS EVENTUALLY GET UNDER WAY

As we have confirmed, the intentions of the London clique were fashioned in 1939-40 when they were unhappy over the groupings in the mini-leagues designed for them by the Football League. In July 1940 they were of a mind to stage a knockout cup for midweek evenings in the month of September. Ambition seemed to override commonsense understanding as availability of daylight amounted to just a couple of weeks. However, the important point was that agitation was already being stirred. Of course prior to the London Cup actually kicking off in 1941 the half season until then had seen all the interested and disinterested parties involved in South Regional League commitments.

From an early stage Crystal Palace seemed to be well on its way to the best goal average record in the area. Though the Glaziers had lost five of 18 games their wins were almost all high scoring affairs with a seven in one and three games in which they scored six times, while defeats were when conceding few goals. They were also able to use only 19 players - three of them being ever present. There were five regulars available and they were one of few London clubs managing to run a youth team in the London Junior Combination. All London clubs had agreed to take part in such a competition for youngsters except Arsenal and Tottenham because since they were sharing a ground there would be no alternative venues available. West Ham had turned down Southend United's appeal to play at Upton Park because it would upset the Hammers plans for their own juniors. Palace with Orient, Fulham and Brentford managed games in this competition though fixtures were spasmodic.

Wartime or not players in first team matches were often serious enough on the pitch and on 28 September when Palace were playing Millwall a penalty was awarded to which the visiting players took exception. Twice the ball was kicked away from the spot and some spectators became involved, too. The referee took the players for a cooling off period and manners were restored. It should be stressed that the wartime innovation of players shaking hands after a match was usually observed in the correct spirit. That same 28 September Brentford had been due to host Chelsea at Griffin Park but an unexploded time bomb in Braemar Road prevented it.

Servicemen who swapped duties with a comrade or war workers who changed shifts in similar circumstances often took on assumed names when playing. These were invariably discovered by the Press and subsequently revealed when any likely repercussions had disappeared. Crystal Palace often found one of their regular goal scorers being referred to as Marksman. It was close enough for Jack Blackman and even a rhyming version for Billy Barke.

West Ham involved in one fewer game than the Glaziers had boosted its goal average quite substantially with an 11-0 win over Southend United with George Foreman scoring four and Stan Foxall getting a hat trick to beach the previously snubbed and now Chelmsford-based Shrimpers. The Hammers had opened the season well enough, too, winning 3-2 at Spurs with veteran centre-half Jim Barrett scoring in the second minute in his 18th season with the club! Arsenal had followed both Glaziers and Hammers in an impressive firing line with twice scoring eight and hitting seven goals in two other matches. On 9 November bomb damage at the Boleyn Ground prevented the visit of Brentford.

On 16 November playing Brentford at Griffin Park, West Ham turned up with nine players. They fared as such for 20 minutes. The Bees loaned them Ray Ferris actually a Linfield wing-half, then Ted Fenton arrived to complete the eleven and the Hammers went on to win 2-0.

The FA having relaxed the rules on "spotters" being posted to scan the skies during air-raid alerts, on 12 October it was announced that all matches must be stopped when the sirens sounded though police were allowed to use their discretion in the circumstances. A couple of weeks later the Ministry of Home Security banned "spotters" though they continued to operate here and there.

Naturally the loss of Charlton Athletic was a blow but one could appreciate its stance. In their nine fixtures at The Valley including both games with Chelsea the total attendances amounted to 6,281. In his club notes manager Jimmy Seed wrote: "Club closes down for duration of war or when conditions make it advisable to restart." On 7 September at The Valley against neighbours Millwall the sirens had begun with a minute left for play. In the raid shrapnel fell on the ground and some women among the crowd sheltering under the stand had to be fortified with whisky from the boardroom! After the interruption with the majority of the crowd gone home, the missing 60 seconds were completed! Subsequently The Valley suffered four high explosives on the terraces, two on the pitch including one on a penalty spot and a direct hit on the ambulance hut.

With local factories working seven days a week, the source of support was meagre. Large scale evacuation of children in the London area and the increase in available manpower directed to the war effort in one way or another restricted the numbers who were available to watch football anyway. Mass Observation revealed that 65% of pre-war Saturday football followers were no longer attending for various wartime reasons.

Charlton had been playing in the second match that season involving a Football League club in which one team had to play a man short. On 30 November both goalkeeper Syd Hobbins and wing-half George Smith failed to reach the ground and the Addicks were forced to play with ten players. John Oakes swapped his centre-half role for the jersey between the posts. Charlton lost 2-1 to West Ham. The Hammers themselves had been forced into a similar situation with ten men against Clapton Orient on 29 September in a 3-3 draw. In instance number three Orient also suffered the ten-man curse when on 21 December against Tottenham they arrived five players adrift. They scratched around and with Spurs lending them one of the Sperrin brothers they also played one short. But it was still a 9-0 drubbing for them.

Reading in Berkshire had achieved slightly better support and had also succeeded in scoring in each one of their 19 South Regional matches. The area was well served with servicemen stationed in fairly close proximity and this helped when signed players were unavailable. As for Spurs they saved their best scoring for the last three games in December beating as mentioned Clapton Orient 9-0, drawing 3-3 with Millwall and taking another seven goals off poor Orient with all three matches played at White Hart Lane. England amateur cap and RAF officer Jackie Gibbons had a hat trick in both Orient matches and one goal against the Lions. On 7 September the air-raid warning ended the 41 win over West Ham in the 80th minute. The official Spurs programme for the Chelsea game on 14 September showed ten changes and included at centre-forward Bobby Sainsbury aged 16 a pre-war junior at the club. The match was interrupted after 15 minutes by another air raid warning but resumed after 80 minutes and Spurs won 3-2. On 12 October before the "really" local derby with Arsenal, Willie Hall was taken ill just before kick-off and Arsenal loaned them their twelfth man Private Les Henley. Spurs lost 3-2 but only 47 minutes was played due to the air raid warning. Then on 23 November a halt was called on 60 minutes for the same reason when leading Luton 2-1. Thus the only three Tottenham wins before December had been when less than 90 minutes had been played! Spurs lost £13,169 that season.

Probably better off than many others for players, Arsenal had the unusual experience of travelling to Northampton on 23 November to find the local team three men short. By half-time the Gunners were seven up and it was only then a call was made to the Cobblers crowd for volunteers and with at last eleven bodies wearing shirts they restricted Arsenal to just one more goal. A week later with Palace visitors to the White Hart Lane based Arsenal the 2-2 draw was watched by 761 spectators with match receipts of £36.

Life was tough for Orient fielding eleven players a major headache each week. Though the London clubs operated a player pool system wherever possible there was no guarantee that those selected would be able to arrive successfully. Even so Orient had started 1940-41 encouragingly enough drawing at Brentford – where they borrowed Ernie Muttitt who scored for them – and then QPR. They also shared six goals with West Ham in the fourth outing before beating Brentford in the return 1-0, though that was to be the only other result in their favour. On 2 November at home to Rangers they had to send a blackboard round the ground calling for any professional footballers to report to the dressing-room! The attendance was only 200 but there were 24 volunteers among them willing to give the game a go! Brentford had four players who did not miss a match until the end of the year but experienced indifferent results and QPR's best performance was beating Arsenal 3-2 on 28 September.

Due to travel to Norwich on 14 September, Rangers only had three players available. The remaining eight were either serving in the Police War Reserve, on munitions or engaged in other essential work and unable to return late for various night shift duties. The game had to be called off. In November Brentford also refused to play at Norwich. City offered a bus with sleeping accommodation but with the uncertainty of the air raids this enterprising idea had to be scrapped.

Oddly enough Chelsea mirrored Spurs in that their last three games in December and it proved their best, too. They won 3-1 at Charlton, 5-2 at home against neighbours Fulham and then took six goals off Aldershot also at Stamford Bridge. The Shots as ever in the period had to rely on whatever Army personnel of quality was in camp and not required for representative games when their own players were elsewhere. Results tended to reflect such varying situations. On 12 October England centre-forward Tommy Lawton fresh from his Army PT course scored three for Aldershot in the 5-1 win over Bristol City.

On the same day Chelsea at Brighton found Albion with five amateurs among its eleven. Some 500 people were inside the ground and an air raid alert ended the proceedings after 55 minutes. A month on and Arsenal had to pull out of a similar visit to the Goldstone Ground. None of their four goalkeepers were attainable, two players were injured and four detailed for an RAF representative game. The same day Brentford leading 4-1 at Charlton suffered a similar early stoppage.

Fulham won only a handful of games, but Millwall had 11 successes and drew four of their 19 but did not play Arsenal once. On 14 September against Crystal Palace the Lions gave a debut to 17 year old Poplar boy Ivor Broadis. Only 40 minutes of play was possible but Broadis made it a scoring winning debut. At least a dozen matches had been interrupted in the period.

Out-of-towners Norwich had beaten a Brighton team containing few of its own players when making the long Christmas Day trip to Carrow Road, completing the numbers with City reserves the odd soldier and a spectator. 18-0 was the final score. Boxing Day and Brentford could not fulfil a fixture at Queen's Park Rangers because the Government refused two consecutive days for football that would have interrupted essential war work.

On 22 December a plea by the Football League to the London clubs for an alternative proposal to prevent the London Cup competition going ahead had been rejected. So much for the background before both A and B groups began in earnest on 4 January 1941 oddly enough with a couple of surprise results involving both winners of the secret ballot that completed the "dirty dozen." In Group A it was a second half goal by Aldershot's own Harry Brooks that took out Chelsea and in Group B an Arsenal team including Ted Drake, Cliff Bastin and the Compton brothers Denis and Leslie in attack lost 2-0 at Reading. First half goals from the amateur international Maurice Edelston and Magnus "Tony" MacPhee pleased most of the 6,158 crowd. The attendance was the highest of the day anywhere in the country.

At Griffin Park, Brentford and Crystal Palace shared four goals but Fulham defeated Queen's Park Rangers 4-1 at Craven Cottage in the other Group A fixtures. In Group B, West Ham United won 2-1 at Millwall and a hat trick from Jackie Gibbons took care of Clapton Orient for Tottenham Hotspur at White Hart Lane. Millwall had been forced to make a late change when Fred Fisher became unavailable and there was no other alternative than for manager Bill Voisey to take the right-wing role. Old "Banger" was a sprightly 50 at the time!

Interesting to note that there were 15 other matches played that day involving Football League clubs mostly regional cup ties but all of them counting in the overall championships for either North or South competitions.

A week on and the London Cup's six games were all return fixtures and went ahead as scheduled. Chelsea took it out on Aldershot easing to a 5-1 win at Stamford Bridge but though Rangers matched this nap hand, Fulham were two goals better with seven in a twelve goal see-saw after Cottagers had been trailing 3-1 at the interval. Crystal Palace and Brentford ended 2-2 at Selhurst Park. Alas Jim Millbank the Palace centre-half and the Bees Doug Hunt were sent off.

However it was Reading who continued to cause a stir by completing a double over Arsenal 1-0 at White Hart Lane, the Gunners having to make six changes, two of them positional, but still including Drake and Leslie Compton. Reading's marksman was Harold Cothliff the Torquay United player whose £6,000 transfer to Chelsea had been scrubbed when war was declared. But the high scoring was at Brisbane Road where Clapton Orient faced a second half barrage from Spurs who had scored twice before the interval and finished 9-1 winners with Gibbons getting another hat trick. Both Ivor Broadis – by now on amateur forms with Spurs – and George Ludford helped themselves to two goals each. Orient struggling to find a goalkeeper was forced to play manager Billy Wright in goal at the last minute. He was nearing 38 years of age. He had been a half-back in his previous playing career with the club.

At Upton Park, West Ham completed a same score double over the Lions though Spurs were leading the table on goal average with maximum points. Fulham headed the Group A table as its only team with four points.

Snow in the southern half on 18 January meant that Brentford v Chelsea was just one of many such casualties. However, Millwall succeeded after arranging to meet Spurs at The Den and lost for the third time in succession. Gibbons only scored twice this time and Broadis added the third after the teams had been level 1-1 in the first half. But all six teams were on duty seven days later.

In Group A Brentford after two drawn matches won with a second half goal from Hunt at Chelsea and Palace who had shared points with the Bees in both opening games surprised Fulham with a 5-2 win, Albert Dawes scoring a hat trick. Fight back time for Aldershot at Loftus Road where Joe Mallett's brace had put Queen's Park Rangers into what appeared a winnable lead, until three goals gave the visitors victory.

Orient did have a recognised goalkeeper in Group B against Reading in Charlie Hillam but Reading still put four goals past him at Brisbane Road, Edelston getting two and Cothliff and MacPhee one each. Spurs carried on their impressive start taking four goals off Millwall to complete a double over the Lions. One of Ludford's two goals took a deflection off John Oakes. At least Arsenal won both points at West Ham winning 3-1 with goals from Drake, Bastin and George Curtis.

Plenty of goals all told in Group A on 1 February. Aldershot and Palace divided six of them equally, Fulham hit Brentford 4-1 and Rangers defeated Chelsea 5-2. The Pensioners had been forced to chop and change each week with new faces and a general switch around of others. Albert Tennant had appeared in both inside-forward positions and on the left-wing, George Smith in all three half-back roles and there had been three different left-backs! Thus Group A was led by Fulham with three wins out of four.

Relief and the plaudits for Clapton Orient for holding Arsenal to a 3-3 draw at Brisbane Road with Johnny McNeil the hat trick hero for them. Leslie Compton, Alf Kirchen and Cliff Bastin replied for the Gunners. McNeil, who was regarded more usually as a centre-half and signed in 1939 from Plymouth, was only one of two personnel changes from the previous week. Unbeaten Reading won 2-0 against the struggling Millwall Lions at The Den who suffered their fifth successive loss. Oddly enough while there had been numerous changes in the forward line, there had been only one in defence and that in the half-back line until this latest reverse. Reading had the services of Frank Swift in goal

A first win, too, for West Ham who inflicted a first defeat on Spurs in the London Cup with goals from Sam Small and long serving Ted Fenton. Moreover Tottenham had lost its place at the head of Group B with Reading leading on goal average having not conceded once and also having a match in hand of their rivals.

On 8 February Group A continued its scoring spree with 23 from the three games. Brentford beat leaders Fulham 7-4, Queen's Park Rangers turned the tables on Aldershot at the Recreation Ground winning 4-2 and Chelsea managed a 3-3 draw at Crystal Palace. Idris Hopkins scored three for Brentford and Eddie Perry had two goals. These two teams were bracketed together on the same number of points but Fulham maintained its leading position by .02 of a goal!

Yet seven days is more than a lifetime in wartime football and not the least for Orient. Just a short while after their heart-warming draw with Arsenal, the return fixture at White Hart Lane was disastrous. Again the main problem position was in goal. This time the unfortunate custodian was MacIlroy with no previous experience in first class football. Arsenal won 15-2 and War Reserve Police Constable Leslie Compton scored ten of the goals, including a hat trick in four minutes at one stage. But McNeil did get on the score sheet again for Orient.

Reading not only dropped its first point of the season but at home and conceded two goals to Millwall after losing a 2-0 lead. Bill Layton from the penalty spot and Johnny Sherwood had salvaged the point. It was the Lions first game without defeat in the Cup campaign, but the Elm Park team retained the lead in Group B because Spurs were beaten 3-2 at West Ham, the Hammers completing a double over the Lilywhites.

Though another goalkeeper was on duty for Reading in the form of young amateur Hubert Penny the half-back line had not been disturbed and two other players had appeared in all five games. So at the half-way stage of the London Cup, Reading was the only undefeated team of the dozen taking part.

Then because its competition took precedence, there was the interruption for the Football League War Cup into which the London clubs were allowed to participate as they were not in any breach of existing rules. There was a regional draw on a home and away basis but it still paired Arsenal at Brighton in the first leg, West Ham at Norwich, Fulham away to Watford and Millwall at Southend (Chelmsford of course). Both Chelsea and Spurs were first leg hosts to Portsmouth and Bournemouth respectively. Since Southampton's ground was out of commission, they were due to play Brentford at Portsmouth's Fratton Park. Aldershot drew Orient away and Reading entertained Bristol City. The only all-London tie involved Crystal Palace v Queen's Park Rangers.

Survivors from the First Round among the London clubs were then paired: Aldershot v QPR, Brentford v Chelsea, Southend v West Ham, Tottenham v Southampton, Reading v Cardiff and Watford v Arsenal. Once the elimination process continued Round Three ties were: QPR v Chelsea, West Ham v Arsenal and Tottenham v Cardiff. At Cardiff a crowd of 18,000 at Ninian Park paid receipts of £1,250.

The three who made it to the quarter-finals were Arsenal, Spurs and QPR. The North London rivals faced each other, but Rangers had to meet out of-town Leicester City. Despite winning the first leg 2-1, Rangers crashed 6-1 at Filbert Street. The first leg at White Hart Lane enabled Arsenal to lead 2-1 before a crowd of 22,107 on 29 March. In the return leg it was drawn 1-1 this time with an attendance of 25,258. The Gunners goalkeeping problems were such that England international Eddie Hapgood played the entire 90 minutes between the sticks.

In the semi-final Arsenal met Leicester and had to take a slender 1-0 lead away but again won 2-1. Into the final held at Wembley on 10 May Denis Compton scored against Preston North End, but his brother Leslie failed with a penalty watched by 60,000. The replay was not until three weeks later on 31 May at Blackburn's Ewood Park and Preston won 2-1. Bobby Beattie's second goal from the start of the second half was scored after six seconds! Preston had been bombarded with ticket requests but considered none from outside the area. The attendance was 45,000 and the communal cup pool already guaranteeing clubs £150 each it was now likely to increase to £160 from this additional match. Just to point out that ground problems also existed outside of London, Preston had played the first half of the season down the road apiece at Leyland Motors.

But of course by this time the London Cup had resumed its activity and when clubs were knocked out of the War Cup remaining fixtures were fitted in. It was rather on the messy side, but then wartime regional fare was renowned for such situations. Tidy it wasn't. The return for the London Cup was on 1 March with a game in each group. Palace's 4-1 Group A win at Fulham was a personal triumph for Bert Robson with all four. Moreover the Glaziers were now in a strong position to finish top. Millwall won 1-0 at Orient in Group B. But it was two weeks before another match and more grief for Fulham beaten 3-1 at Aldershot. Albert Dawes whose post-dated cheque for his transfer from Palace to the Shots had been cancelled on the outbreak of war, returned to the Recreation Ground and scored twice for them! However, he was still registered by the Football League as a Shots player.

One imagined it could not get much worse for Fulham but it did. On 22 March with Fulham concerned that the Craven Cottage gate would be hit by QPR's League War Cup tie with neighbours Chelsea the return with Aldershot was given permission to be back in Hampshire and another 4-2 reverse. Dawes was again on the score sheet. The significance of the result was that though they had now played more matches than any other Group A team, Aldershot with nine points from seven matches were top. Brentford was second two points behind but significantly possessed two games in hand. The same day two Group B ties saw Arsenal win 6-1 at Millwall with a Leslie Compton hat trick among the goals and Reading obtaining another point in a 1-1 draw at West Ham.

On 29 March Brentford and Chelsea shared four goals at Griffin Park but Hunt was again off for an early bath. After the match the Bees skipper was censured for not insisting one of his players accept the referee's decision and resume play. The FA decided that under their jurisdiction: "a team captain is responsible for the collective conduct of his players and failure will lead to disciplinary action against him and the club." Clubs were instructed to inform their captains accordingly.

Reading confirmed their Group B standing with luckless Orient on the wrong end of nine goals. Tony MacPhee had a four-timer. Seven days later the crunch game came at Griffin Park with Brentford entertaining Aldershot. Leading 1-0 at half-time the Bees eventually won 4-2 with Hopkins and Perry each scoring twice. Palace won 3-1 at Chelsea to keep alive their group title hopes and semi-final confirmation. Reading defeated West Ham 4-1 and with Fred Reeve scoring a hat trick for Millwall they added another four goals to Orient's "against" column.

On 12 April Brentford drew 2-2 at Aldershot, Queen's Park Rangers won 2-1 at Palace to the disappointment of the home crowd and Fulham at last found some form with a 4-0 drubbing of neighbours Chelsea. Over in Group B another pasting for Orient conceding an 8-1 defeat at West Ham for whom even defenders Alf Chalkley and Norman Corbett got on the scorers list. There were even Easter Monday matches slotted in. Brentford cemented their position leading in Group A with a 4-2 victory against QPR and a Robson goal for Palace was sufficient to take care of Aldershot at Selhurst Park. One Group B game and Reading drew 2-2 at Spurs having led 2-0 at the interval.

Chelsea managed a revenge win over Fulham on 19 April at Stamford Bridge winning 4-3. Fred Kurz who had missed the defeat at Craven Cottage was back and scored twice while Rooke had another couple for the visitors. Though erroneously reported in some sources that the ubiquitous Dawes had hit both goals for Queen's Park Rangers in a 21 win against Palace, the QPR saviour had been Jock Davie the Brighton centre-forward with a brace. Palace's hopes of runners-up position and a semi-final chance now rested on Rangers who still had two matches to play but needed substantial scoring wins to achieve an outside possibility.

In Group B, Orient was able to put a better eleven on view and though holding West Ham to a 1-1 draw at half-time were edged out 3-2 at the final whistle. The Hammers late spurt was unlikely to reap runners-up reward. Reading was held 2-2 at Elm Park by Tottenham, but enough to prevent being overtaken. The point was equally valuable for Spurs. There was only one game in Group A on 26 April a goalless draw between Rangers and Brentford at Loftus Road. Highly competitive was probably an understatement for what went on. Brentford winger Leslie Smith had his jaw broken in three places! Though the Rangers defender Ted Reay was not sent off he was subsequently suspended for seven months. However the point was enough to land the group leadership to the Griffin Park club and a place in the semi-final. At the same time of course it was the end of any forlorn hopes of Rangers snatching second place in front of Palace.

On 3 May Group A was wound up with Rangers belatedly winning 3-2 at Chelsea. Davie was again on the mark for them and Dave Mangnall scored twice to take his tally to eight in the London Cup. To Chelsea it was the wooden spoon. Brentford and Palace were semi-finalists. Meanwhile Group B was still behind with four outstanding fixtures and Reading poised as group champions in waiting. Spurs and Arsenal continued to be in with a shout for a semi-final place, the Gunners best placed appearing in all four games because of their extended League War Cup exploits, Spurs in two of them, their local derbies! Alas for Arsenal its "other" cup final was only seven days away.

Since both teams were at "home" at White Hart Lane it was Spurs with the "advantage." A crowd of 9,651 watched an entertaining 3-3 draw which gave Arsenal a decided edge, with the proviso of the looming Wembley event. The Gunners fielded: Boulton; Drake (at right-back), Scott, Henley, Joy, Collett, Kirchen, Lewis, Leslie Compton, Beasley and Nelson. Leslie Compton was on target with two goals. As previously referred to, he crucially missed from the penalty spot on 10 May, when Arsenal used Marks, Hapgood, Crayston, Bastin, Leslie Jones and Denis Compton in a much-changed line-up.

Fate was now casting a shadow over Arsenal. Long before the replayed final with Preston was lost of course the return with Spurs had to be played and prior to that on 17 May Leslie Compton did register from a penalty in Group B when Arsenal beat West Ham 3-0, Drake scoring the other two goals. This gave the Gunners ten points. On 21 May with another different line-up Arsenal it was the crucial return with Tottenham one point ahead. But Arsenal lost 3-0 in front of 6,673 spectators and Spurs who now had 13 points from their ten games were safely second with a semi-final to come. Three days later Arsenal won 5-2 at Millwall but could only finish fourth. Drake with three goals took his London Cup tally to six, almost a third of Leslie Compton's 17. At left-back Arsenal had Andy Beattie as a guest who was to appear for Preston his own club against them a week later!

It was the replay of the League Cup Final on 31 May and the same day the semi-finals of the London Cup were also played. Reading winners of Group B were drawn at home to Crystal Palace the runners-up in Group A, while Group B runners-up Tottenham Hotspur played Group A winners Brentford at White Hart Lane. It would have been a fairer pairing if both group champions had been granted a home game, but the luck of the draw is the great gamble.

Reading raced to a 3-1 lead by half-time and won 4-1 with the skipper Tony MacPhee scoring another treble. The Elm Park attendance was 5,303. At Spurs two second half goals gave Brentford an unexpected victory in front of 6,495. With the season already extended into June the final between Reading and Brentford was held a week later on 7 June at Stamford Bridge. With a somewhat erratic display by George Poland the Brentford goalkeeper Reading just edged the game 3-2 after the players had gone in at half-time level at 1-1. Eddie Perry had given the Bees the advantage but Johnny Sherwood had equalized. Wilf Chitty put Reading ahead only for Perry to level it before Maurice Edelston, son of the Reading manager Joe Edelston scored the winning goal for Reading.

The cup was handed to MacPhee by A V Alexander First Lord of the Admiralty and the attendance was reported at 9,000 with receipts amounting to £580. There were no medals handed out, the players were each rewarded with a 7s.6d Savings Certificate. MacPhee, a player with precision near goal had started the war making eye pieces for gas marks.

Naturally in the weeks leading up to the climax of the London Cup there were Saturdays when more South Regional League matches could be added. Some of the London clubs even ventured to play teams outside the region perhaps smoothing the way to some one day reconciliation Fulham even trekked to Norwich but lost 2-0 but with a Ronnie Rooke hat trick then achieved a 3-3 draw at Portsmouth. Millwall had home and away games with Northampton but lost both 4-1 at the Den and 5-1 at the County Ground. Chelsea also went to Northampton and suffered a 4-1 defeat. But Chelsea did get to play Arsenal at Stamford Bridge on Easter Monday, the only time the two clubs met that season. They even won 3-1.

On 22 March Crystal Palace was beating Brentford 4-0 when they were awarded a penalty. The Bees goalkeeper George Duke was unhappy with the decision and walked off, followed by the referee and both teams. After a cooling off period the players minus Duke returned and Arthur Hudgell made it 5-0 from the penalty spot.

On 10 May, a week before defeat at Northampton, Chelsea even ventured "abroad" visiting Cardiff City at Ninian Park and won 2-1 with Dickie Spence and Fred Kurz scoring. A week later it was Spurs turn for a midlands trip to Leicester rewarded by a 2-1 win. Ronnie Burgess scored twice and the following week Tottenham won the return 3-0.

Alas the season entered into farce when the Football League decided to give the disaffected southern teams - their noses put out by the London Cup - a little competition of their own. From 11 January 1941 all matches played by Bournemouth, Brighton, Luton, Norwich, Portsmouth, Southampton, Southend and Watford were to be competed for in the Football League South. Yet there was confusion as some reports indicated that neither Luton nor Norwich were among the original choice. Despite points being awarded for wins and a draw, all these results would also be included in the South Regional League where the goals for and against were the primary object! Needless to mention the travelling required to complete these matches was considerable. The London clubs might even have made the point that it was against the Government edict: "Is your journey really necessary?"

There had been some spectacular individual scoring achievements. Bert Barlow hit six for Portsmouth in the 10-2 win over Bournemouth including a hat trick in three and a half minutes, while Charlton's Don Welsh also had a six-timer when Brighton beat Luton 7-4 on 22 March.

On 3 May Brighton defeated Watford 4-2. It was then announced that the team leading the Football League South table would be declared champions, but that neither Luton nor Norwich's results would be included because these two clubs had not played in the opening weeks!

If the results of Luton and Norwich were omitted Brighton would have taken 14 points from their first ten matches. For Watford minus these factors its total was 15.

Including the matches against Luton and Norwich it remained Watford 15 Brighton 13. Understand, too, that on 3 May it was either Brighton's eleventh or 13th game and Watford should have been declared champions. Even so Brighton protested and a play-off took place on 31 May – at Brighton! They won 4-1 and were declared champions of Football League South. The final table excluding this match placed Brighton top with 19 points from 13 games, Watford second with 17 from 14.

The oddity of goal average separating teams in a League table was compounded at the close when there were three matches counting in the South Regional League listing where the teams involved requested these results to be omitted. On 17 May Aldershot had been involved with the oddest of affairs in the Hants Senior Cup semi-final with Portsmouth while on 2 June Pompey had beaten Southampton 8-1 in the final of the competition. That Regional League South play-off involving Brighton and Watford was other fixture mentioned to be deleted.

As to the Aldershot-Portsmouth cup semi-final at Fratton Park the Shots led 3-1 at the interval were 4-1 up early in the second half but after 90 minutes it was 5-5! Extra time and Portsmouth ran riot scoring another handful to win 10-5! Lawton was playing and scoring a goal for the Shots. Little wonder they were grateful to have the result removed from the table if not the memory of it.

London clubs fared reasonably well in the final South Regional League reckoning. Crystal Palace scored almost twice as many goals as conceded 86 to 44 to finish top on 1.954. Only Preston in the North Regional League had a better average at 2.189. West Ham were placed second in the south, Arsenal fourth and Reading sixth. Spurs and Millwall were tenth and eleventh respectively, the others not in the first half of the listing and Clapton Orient bottom having just one victory and not arranging any such matches except for their two cup tournament commitments in the New Year.

On 22 April the club was suspended for failure to meet "certain obligations." They were reinstated four days later apparently after rectifying these. Orient had previously been rebuffed for ignoring regulations about obtaining players from the crowd! One wonders if the authorities were always aware of existing wartime conditions at all.

Naturally the guest player system was flourishing and never better illustrated – or exploited - than on 7 June the last day of the extended season. Queen's Park Rangers borrowed nine players: four from Chelsea, two from Arsenal plus one each from Crystal Palace, Huddersfield and Oldham. Of course these people were not shipped in from their clubs, just handily in the vicinity involved as they were on various essential duty and war work. Rangers won 3-2 at West Ham with Leslie Compton of the Gunners firing another two goals. It took the Arsenal player's haul for the season to 52 of which 42 were with his own club, eight in representative games and the two as a Rangers guest.

Of course finance was a concern or rather for the lack of it. Crystal Palace lost £2,142, West Ham £1,911 and Chelsea £1,429. The FA itself suffered a £9,827 deficit but the Football League reported a modest profit of £16! But charity benefited and the Red Cross fund was boosted through the game to £18,282.

THEN LONDON CLUBS BECOME SERIOUS

The London Cup might not have entirely captured the imagination of the football public in 1940-41 but it had been completed – even fitted in between other fixtures - and at least encouraged the organizers to flex their muscles more in adopting a League competition of their own. At a meeting of southern clubs chaired by George Allison in July 1941 it was agreed that the list of fixtures submitted by the Football League for the Metropolitan clubs in 1941-42 was unsatisfactory. They stated an intention to proceed with a programme of their own.

The reason given was an inability to undertake the journeys involved which might include visits to Southend (actually Chelmsford), Southampton, Bournemouth, Luton, Swansea and Norwich. For an odd reason neither Portsmouth nor Brighton was mentioned, but the general tone of the refusal was plain enough.

Thereupon the Football League Management Committee made the following pronouncement for the League Competition 1941-42: "Whereas at a duly convened meeting of the members of the League held in Nottingham on 9 June 1941, it was unanimously agreed and resolved that a League Championship competition in two sections North and South with fixtures made by the League be instituted and whereas in compliance with that resolution the Management Committee of the League have compiled and issued to the members fixtures made by them, having due regard to the circumstances and the just claims of all members and whereas the members set out below have intimated their intention to retire from this competition … (*Clearly brevity and any nodding acquaintance with grammar did not feature in this legalise agenda*).

"The Management Committee have given due consideration to such decision and consider it necessary to direct the attention of those members to the Articles of Association of the Football League and in particular to Articles 8 and 15 (c) thereof.

"The Management Committee have therefore resolved that such withdrawal shall not be accepted and call upon the clubs proposing to take part in football to fulfil the obligations voluntarily entered into and unless the clubs concerned shall on or before 2 August 1941 notify the Secretary of their compliance with this decision, the Management Committee will have no alternative but to put into operation the Articles of Association above referred to, the effect of which is that the non-complying clubs would cease to be members of the Football League:-

"Aldershot, Arsenal, Brentford, Charlton Athletic, Chelsea, Clapton Orient, Crystal Palace, Fulham, Millwall Athletic, Queen's Park Rangers, Reading, Tottenham Hotspur, West Ham United, Crewe Alexandra."

Of course the London rebels had no wish or intention to include Crewe in their scheme, but since that club had stated they would play in the Northern Section but not the Southern, the Football League had made the decision to lump them in with the London clique. Additionally there were other measures taken over the cancellation of shares.

Shortly afterwards Brighton and Watford resigned and joined the London group making effectively 15, at least one short of a satisfactory number of teams for a suitable competition. On 5 August the Football League announced that all 15 had ceased to be members of the Football League and cancelled the shares of the eight full members namely

Arsenal, Brentford, Charlton, Chelsea, Fulham, Millwall, Tottenham and West Ham. Then on 11 August Portsmouth joined the rebels making a manageable 16 and guaranteeing 30 fixtures with a group stage cup to follow. Pompey was actually elected as there had been other undisclosed applicants!

This produced some backtracking by the Football League with a softening of the wording and "expulsion" being replaced by "suspension." Entreaties to the The League's Appeals Committee consisting of such laudable people as C Wreford Brown, B A Glanvill and H J Husband were made on behalf of the London group and the League agreed for these to go forward without admitting any right of appeal. It should be noted that the gentlemen in question were primarily outstanding figures in the Football Association's sphere.

Fearing its authority was likely to be undermined by this apparent retreat, the Football League pointed out that any subsequent return to the fold might mean Full Members like Arsenal and Chelsea having to win promotion from the depths of the Third Division. But the unlikelihood of a shortening of the war rendered this a harmless gesture. However, the League's South fixtures had to be rearranged and might well have involved extensive travel, precisely the point behind the London group's stance. Even so Swansea being faced with the prospect of venturing across country to Norwich was not a remote possibility.

An eleventh-hour compromise failed despite meetings in Derby and London during the third week of August. Even on the eve of the new season the London groups own appeal to the League's Appeal Board was still waiting to be heard! The London League began on 30 August. Incidentally poor Crewe did not compete at all! With more clubs opting out but others returning to the fold the Football League's strength was down to 51, the lowest figure since the Great War.

Strangely enough the Football League had shown flexibility in 1940-41 by allowing three non-league clubs to be co-opted into a Western Regional League to help Bristol City, Cardiff and Swansea to have some reasonably local competition. Even this had problems. Swansea withdrew and Cardiff Corinthians replaced them. A widening of this scheme would have benefited other outlying areas, particularly the unique case of isolated Norwich City. This policy was sensibly to be carried on again from 1942-43 for the League West with Swansea back and Aberaman Athletic, Bath City and Lovells Athletic again involved.

While the unsatisfactory goal average system was dropped by the Football League there had to be a percentage of points adopted for the truncated 1941-42 South region in view of the probability of unfulfilled fixtures. The figures were calculated over 18 games though of the 13 teams only two managed to complete as many as 18. Needless to say the clubs making up this Baker's Dozen were not best pleased with the attitude of the London clique.

The London League insured 12 players for every club under better terms than the Football League. A sum of £500 was paid on death or permanent disablement, for partial disablement £2 a week for 52 weeks. The London Junior Combination was started involving Brentford, Chelsea, Clapton Orient, Crystal Palace, Fulham, Millwall, Queen's Park Rangers and West Ham United. Arsenal and Tottenham Hotspur with White Hart

Lane fully occupied could not include a team. Kit for all remained a concern. At the time jerseys and shorts required five clothing coupons each, stockings three and boots seven.

On 30 August the 16 teams opened the London League programme. The League North had 19 fixtures, League South just five. But the rebels' competition produced a shock result. Arsenal featuring six of their pre-war internationals lost 4-1 at Brentford conceding three goals in the second half. Griffin Park's attendance was estimated at 12,000 a figure only equalled that day for the Lancashire derby between Preston North End and Blackpool.

Forty-five goals were scored, Reading won 8-3 at Clapton Orient with a Maurice Edelston hat trick and the quickest goal scored in the London League in the first minute by Jack Bradley for Reading, the *Reading Standard* having refuted the scorers and their order reported elsewhere that day. Aldershot won 6-2 at Fulham. Tommy Lawton had scored twice against Stan Cullis in the Shots trial match the previous week. He hit another couple against the England centre-half who was Fulham's No.5! Queen's Park Rangers arrived at Brighton a player short and the Seagulls loaned Army PT instructor Jock Davie to them. Bad move. He swooped to score three times in a 5-2 win. Charlton's match with Chelsea at The Valley had a 6 pm kick-off to allow war workers to attend after their various shifts. The crowd was 6,793. Don Welsh scored twice for the Addicks who had 17 year-old Stanley Gibbs at inside-right in the 2-1 win.

The following Saturday there were more goals 58 in all with only Orient failing to score at least one. Reg Lewis leading the Arsenal attack had a nap hand including two in four minutes in the 7-2 win over Crystal Palace and West Ham United won a game of twelve goals at Stamford Bridge doubling Chelsea's foursome. On 13 September Lewis had a treble in the 5-2 win at Fulham with the Craven Cottage crowd numbering 10,473. As a youngster Lewis sold score cards at The Oval. The Portsmouth-Aldershot match at Fratton Park was abandoned in the 77th minute at 2-2 with a broken goalpost the result of Andy Black crashing into the net while scoring. The result stood.

Seven days later the season's first landlord-lodgers affair at White Hart Lane saw Arsenal "at home" take four goals off Tottenham Hotspur without reply. A 17,446 gate was easily the highest anywhere in the country. But Arsenal reported a loss of £6,000 from the previous season. Best individual scorers were Magnus MacPhee with five of Reading's in the 6-2 win over Crystal Palace and Ronnie Rooke getting four in Fulham's 5-2 success at Queen's Park Rangers. League leaders Brentford dropped their first point of the season in a 2-2 draw at Brighton. Sid Cann missed a penalty for Charlton but they still beat Watford 5-1.

On 27 September, bottom of the table Watford had yet to scrape a point and this fifth attempt was the poorest thus far with West Ham scoring eight without reply at Vicarage Road. Seven goals came in the second half. Now into their stride Arsenal attract 15,785 at Portsmouth and Lewis with another two goals took his total to twelve in Pompey's first defeat. Shortly afterwards it was reported that Portsmouth had suffered a loss of £284 on the previous season. Chelsea's games often attracted goals but their treble at Millwall was only half of the Lions share. The Orient manager Billy Wright had to play centre-half in their 3-1 reverse against Brentford.

But previously undefeated Brentford lost its record when Crystal Palace went to Griffin Park to win 2-1. Arsenal took over at the top following the 3-0 whitewash of Chelsea at White Hart Lane. Watford secured their first point in sharing four goals with Orient at Vicarage Road. Modest scoring all round on that 4 October just 25 in the eight matches. But Watford came down to earth a week later at the Recreation Ground as Aldershot thumped them 8-1. Lawton had a hat trick and Hagan scored twice. Brentford were edged out 4-3 at Fulham but Arsenal maintained its lead winning 3-1 at Charlton watched by 13,910. The Valley car park was filled with civilian and military vehicles as well as youthful autograph hunters! With six of their Liverpool guests Brighton stunned Spurs at White Hart Lane 2-1, one of the sextet Jack Balmer scoring both Seagulls goals. Balmer and Phil Taylor were accomplished tank drivers, too.

The 18 October results saw Arsenal stretch its advantage to three points in beating West Ham 4-1 at "home" as Brentford lost 4-1 at Griffin Park to Spurs and Portsmouth slipped up 2-1 along the coast at Brighton. The Albion had not lost since the opening day and had 11 points from their eight games. The Hammers had similarly suffered a second reverse. With Crystal Palace beating Fulham 3-1 at Selhurst Park, the Glaziers, Brighton, West Ham and Portsmouth were bracketed together. Lewis had scored in each of the Gunners' victories. The Palace programme listed "Marksman" at No.10. He proved to be Billy Barke. A different "Lawton" in Millwall colours scored once and a Freddie Fisher treble saw Watford beaten 4-2, Dennis Westcott their double striker.

However, the unexpected shock was on 25 October when Arsenal slumped at Watford losing 3-1, in the home side's first win of the season! Significantly Lewis was absent in a team containing several changes though Ted Drake wore the No 9 shirt in Lewis' absence. Yet there were extenuating circumstances. The Gunners trundled on for the kick-in 18 minuets late with only eight men! During it the remaining three arrived. Clearly the upset was a contributory factor. Even so it was not enough for Watford to catch Orient at the foot of the table as a George Willshaw brace of goals saw the East Londoners record their first win too, clipping Fulham 2-1. Wins for Brighton with a Davie hat trick in the 3-1 at Chelsea, Portsmouth beating Brentford 2-1 and West Ham's 2-0 success over Queen's Park Rangers cut the Gunners lead to a point. Reading won 3-2 at Charlton with a late penalty by Bradley. More Pompey goalmouth trouble when Brentford claimed Bill Rochford's second goal for the home team had entered the net from outside it. Referee Robbins allowed the goal to Brentford protests. He stopped the game but play resumed after a touchline conference. Jimmy Guthrie then fired a penalty wide with Portsmouth players amusingly claiming it had gone through the same net! Brentford still lost 2-1.

With a third of the fixtures completed *Status Quo* on 1 November. Lewis back in action and scoring once in the 3-2 win over Aldershot at White Hart Lane, the chief contenders all suffered reverses. Brighton lost 5-3 at the Goldstone to Charlton, whose coach *en route* hit a telegraph pole, the players shaken but unhurt and clearly recovered well!

Portsmouth also beaten 3-1 at Crystal Palace and the Hammers edged out 3-2 at Elm Park where Harold Cothliff scored in under ten seconds from the kick-off for Reading. Even so Watford kept in the headlines in a personal triumph for Wolves' Westcott still on Army leave from Iceland scoring all five in the club's 5-1 success at

Rangers. Orient obtained a point at Millwall for whom Sidney Gibson, 18, had impressed at centre-half, leaving Chelsea bottom with four just points after losing 3-1 at Brentford. Joe James even scored with a header from the half-way line against Chelsea's international goalkeeper Johnny Jackson. Millwall's Sidney Gibson, 18 impressed at centre-half. However, Palace was emerging as a threat two points behind Arsenal.

Arsenal dropped another point in the 2-2 draw at Millwall but had again been forced into more changes though Lewis failed to find the net this time. The start was delayed by 15 minutes with many of an estimated 15,000 crowd attempting to gain entry. An SOS was sent out to the local Greyhound Stadium for extra gate men and eight recruits were enlisted. Tommy Lawton took the individual scoring honours on 8 November with all four for Aldershot in the 4-1 win over Rangers. The Shots were now on 14 points. But Palace slipped up to a Billy Wrigglesworth goal for Chelsea, the Pensioners only third win of the season.

Lewis back finding the net with a hat trick and Leslie Compton restored to the attack getting the other two, Orient was beaten 5-2. Arsenal had already had to use 24 different players. Queen's Park Rangers achieved its third win beating Millwall 4-1 while Chelsea by the same score won again this time at neighbours Fulham. Reading and Aldershot shared six goals at Elm Park but Brentford collapsed in the second half against visiting West Ham conceding four after trailing 1-0 at the break.

The Bees demise lasted but seven days as with Eddie Perry getting a four-timer, Brentford won 6-1 at Watford. Palace also pulled off an unexpected 5-0 win at West Ham. A surprise programme alteration had Albert Dawes not brother Fred at full-back for the Glaziers. Charlton and Fulham shared six goals at The Valley. Arsenal had to start with ten players against Rangers owing to the late arrival of goalkeeper Ted Platt. Drake took over for 15 minutes and kept a clean sheet in the 4-1 win. Orient could only scrape nine men for the visit of Portsmouth who had fortunately brought two spare players with them. Pompey won 4-0. Spurs drew 1-1 at Stamford Bridge but Derby County's Dave McCulloch missed a penalty for Chelsea

On 29 November, Palace struck Watford 6-1, Barke again listed as "Marksman" scoring twice while Brentford beat Aldershot 5-1. Brighton was another with a nap hand delivery over Millwall. The Seagulls gave a left-back debut to Reg Bowles at 15 years 258 days who did well opposing the Lions right-winger the fine flying Fisher. Chelsea still in winning mode 3-2 at Portsmouth and Lewis had two in the 3-1 Gunners win against Reading taking his total so far to 22 goals. A week later Lewis was absent at Brighton but the Gunners won 3-2 with Drake getting on the score sheet. The crowd at the Goldstone was estimated at 10,000. Andy Black had four goals for Portsmouth in the 7-2 win over Charlton taking his total to 18 and Orient won its second game 3-1 at Chelsea.

It was unlucky 13th of December for Arsenal even with Lewis leading the line beaten at "home" 3-1 by Brentford. Pre-war the Bees often had the edge over the Gunners in the First Division. Another international guest sparked Aldershot. Albert Geldard had three telling strikes in the 4-3 clipping of Fulham, Lawton getting the other goal. There was also a fourth success for Rangers 3-0 against Brighton with Dave Mangnall scoring twice. The visitors were forced to make a late change giving 18 year old Jack Ball the goalkeeper's jersey and moving regular custodian Gordon Mee to the wing! Unusually three other teams failed to find the net: Orient, Palace and West Ham.

The Palace fixture against Arsenal was fogged off the list on 20 December and the mist called a halt at Orient after 57 minutes when 1-1 with Charlton, though the score was allowed to stand. Several of the challengers took advantage of the Gunners inactivity. Portsmouth hit seven against Watford with Black getting a hat trick, the visitors having to borrow a player. West Ham scored five against Chelsea and Brentford trimmed neighbours Rangers by the odd goal in seven. Pompey moved just two points adrift of Arsenal. With a hat trick before half-time and a fourth to edge out Millwall 4-3, the Cottagers Ronnie Rooke celebrated his promotion from RAF Corporal to Sergeant with a four-timer.

Christmas Day the White Hart Lane crowd numbered 10,578 for Fulham's visit to the Gunners. Lewis and Alf Kirchen scored in Arsenal's 2-0 win while two down at Aldershot by half-time Portsmouth lost 3-2. West Ham also dropped a point at the Boleyn in a 2-2 draw with Charlton watched by 9,789 and a Trevor Smith treble enabled Crystal Palace to win 3-1 at Queen's Park Rangers. Ivor Broadis who had made a teenage debut for Millwall the previous season returned to The Den but this time had both goals for Spurs in their 2-1 finish.

Another full programme for Saturday two days later and Arsenal won their "away" game at Tottenham 2-1. Drake and Denis Compton were the marksmen before 16,777. Orient achieved its third win 3-1 over West Ham and another two goals for Black helped Portsmouth edge Millwall 3-2. Chelsea surprised Aldershot at the Rec with an odd goal in five win as did Rangers in a three-goal whitewash of Fulham at the Cottage.

There was a double-figure shellacking of a weakened Brighton for Crystal Palace marksmen on 3 January, 10-1 the final tally with Bert Robson on a four-timer and braces for Albert Dawes, Ian Gillespie and Smith. Arsenal also dealt a significant blow to Portsmouth 6-1 at White Hart Lane before a gate of 10,160. Lewis had a second-half trio in less than 15 minutes and Kirchen a brace of goals. Pompey was minus the free-scoring Black. With a coach driver unused to the route, Aldershot arrived 15 minutes late at Charlton. Because of the delayed kick-off only 40 minutes was played each way. Still the Shots won 5-1! Hat tricks for Hammers' Jackie Wood in the 4-1 win against Watford and all three for Millwall's Johnny Osborne in sharing six goals at Chelsea.

Another West Ham treble-shooter a week later was Eddie Chapman, 18, at Aldershot in part of the 5-1 result. Leslie Compton led the Arsenal forwards with Lewis absent and scored twice as Chelsea lost at home 5-1. Though Albert Day had a couple of goals for Brighton, it was more of a day out for the Fulham forwards there. Jack Finch, Pat Gallacher and Ronnie Rooke each scored twice in the 7-3 win. Black back scoring for Pompey as Rangers lost there 3-1. Portsmouth had Royal Marines Ranner deputising in goal.

A Kirchen hat trick on 17 January was crucial as Arsenal edged Charlton 3-2 but Portsmouth slumped 5-2 at Reading where Southampton's Bradley hit four goals. Brighter Brighton as the Albion rattled home 5-2 to complete a double against Spurs with incidentally Arsenal's Stan Morgan proving the menace with three of their goals. A second successive home win for Clapton Orient saw Palace the sufferers letting in four without reply. Sadly there were to be no more such home or away for the Os.

Seven days on in a curtailed programme Arsenal with a fairly representative side on duty crashed 3-0 at West Ham, the attendance reported as 20,000. It was a special occasion as the *Internationale* was played for the first time at a football ground in the country and a collection was taken for Mrs Churchill's Aid to Russia Fund. Orient let in five against Aldershot at Brisbane Road and Pompey won the south coast affair with Brighton 5-3.

On 31 January the Gunners stormed to an 11-0 trouncing of Watford, awful revenge for their defeat at Vicarage Road earlier in the season. Lewis had five goals while doubles came the way of Cliff Bastin, Leslie Compton and Kirchen. Lewis was not alone with his nap hand as Davie hit five for Brighton as they beat Chelsea 8-2. Davie arrived late and actually missed the kick-off, but still managed two goals before half-time. Don Welsh scored three as Charlton won 4-1 at Reading. Black and Bert Barlow had two goals apiece in Portsmouth's 5-2 win at Brentford.

Double-figures one week, none the next that was occasionally the wartime concept and Arsenal were no exception to the unusual times as they lost 1-0 in a first ever visit to Aldershot before a crowd of 8,700. The Shots had ten guest players and George Raynor, Lawton was the scorer mid-way through the second half. Ten goals flooded The Valley but visiting Brighton had only two of them and Charlton's eight included a Charlie Revell hat trick. Jack Court a Cardiff forward stole Black's limelight and shirt for Portsmouth with all three goals against Crystal Palace in the 3-1 win. But inclement weather caused four postponements. Such weather statements could not be broadcast – just witnessed. Even so, Spurs' Jackie Gibbons was able to help Chelsea out in the absence of Albert Tennant and scored their goal in the 1-1 draw with Brentford.

Yes, it was Millwall who had to pay the price for the Gunners misfiring at the Recreation Ground. Four-goal Lewis led the ten-goal Valentine's Day slaughter with a Nelson treble two Bastin penalties and a goal from Les Henley adding to the target. Portsmouth had a 7-2 win at Fulham with Barlow taking three goals and Barnsley's George Bullock getting a couple. Jackie Gibbons had all three for Spurs in the 3-2 result at Orient and double strikes for Maurice Edelston and Magnus MacPhee saw Reading defeat Watford 5-1.

On 21 February it was Watford the surprising highest scorers 7-1 against Brighton. The censor listed one of the scorers as "A Newman" presumably because Artillery man Fred Kurz the player given the alias should have been on duty somewhere else! Brighton's borrowed left-winger was the son of the Watford club's President! Only two goals for Lewis this time as Arsenal won 3-1 at Orient. Fulham won the South West London affair at Chelsea 5-1.

A week on and the accolade as the highest scorers in the London League went to Portsmouth against luckless Orient already 6-1 down at the break they let in another ten in the second half! In the 16-1 score Andy Black had eight goals. In fairness the O's arrived at Fratton Park without a goalkeeper and appeals to the crowd brought an Army recruit called Hedges from the Royal Army Ordnance Corps, clearly ill-equipped for the awesome task confronting him. George Tadman with four goals and Harold Hobbis with three took Charlton to a 7-4 win at Fulham and though Watford held Brentford 3-3 at half-time they lost 5-3 at Griffin Park. Hagan had a hat trick In Aldershot's 5-1 win at Brighton. A second half Drake effort gave Arsenal another two points at Queen's Park Rangers as they closed in on the Championship.

It was achieved at Reading on 7 March in their 28th League game before an estimated crowd of 10,000 producing receipts of £678. Leading 1-0 at half-time Arsenal won 4-1 with Lewis adding to his formidable total with just a couple of goals, Nelson and Denis Compton completing the scoring. Oddly enough on the same afternoon at Stamford Bridge Denis' brother Leslie Compton was helping out Chelsea against Portsmouth but putting through his own goal to give Portsmouth a 4-3 win! Brentford forward Len Townsend's hat trick for Chelsea was of little avail. Orient's goalkeeping woes continued at home to Queen's Park Rangers. Boss Billy Wright again took over between the posts and they only lost 2-1.

Meanwhile Townsend's own club Brentford were on the wrong end of a 6-3 score at Aldershot with Sergeant Instructor Jack Martin, pre-war schoolmaster and Aston Villa part-timer getting a treble in his only outing for the Shots.

From 14 March onwards the interest was in the runners-up race and the other minor places before the start of the Cup competition. Portsmouth the favourites for second spot clinched it with Black and Barlow grabbing a brace apiece as they won 5-2 at Charlton. It was their seventh win in an unbeaten eight-game run to give them 42 points as West Ham albeit with a game in hand, faltered 3-2 at home to Spurs who had been improving too late in the shadow of their Arsenal tenants. The Hammers could only now reach 39 points. Aldershot inflicted Crystal Palace's first home defeat 2-1 after Charlie Briggs saved a late Albert Dawes penalty. Then in what was only his eleventh League game of the season for Arsenal, Drake hit all four goals in the 4-2 win against Brighton. There were still ten League games outstanding when the London War Cup opened on 21 March and these had to be fitted in when the group games had been completed.

But the real news was released on 2 April confirming the mutinous London area clubs had agreed to apologise in writing to the Football League for their rebellious conduct. On the payment of £10 per club they would be reinstated to the fold.

Back on the field of play on 25 April three of these missing London League fixtures were played on the day of the first cup semi-final. Aldershot won 5-1 at Watford and both Spurs and West Ham had 2-1 home wins against Brentford and Reading respectively. The Shots had finished their programme dropping only one point in seven games. But it was West Ham who grabbed third place above them on goal average with a slightly better defensive record than Aldershot.

A week later four more fixtures were knocked off on the second semi-final occasion. Tottenham unusually among the goals scored seven at the expense of Fulham. Gibbons, George Ludford and Leslie Stevens each scored twice. They had drawn two and won six of their last eight to finish in fifth place a point off fourth. Queen's Park Rangers had a rare away win 5-0 at Watford but Clapton Orient ended a nightmare run of seven successive defeats by holding Millwall to a 3-3 draw at Brisbane Road.

On 9 May two more outstanding games saw Arsenal share six goals at Crystal Palace with Lewis' hat trick taking him to 42 League goals in only 23 appearances. Watford beat Millwall but stayed bottom. The last fixture was not played until 23 May when Fulham defeated Crystal Palace 4-3, Jack Conley with a four-timer for the Cottagers.

THE LONDON WAR CUP 1941-42

The 16 teams were drawn in four groups with just the winners moving on to the semifinals. Ironically for a competition whose thesis was the prevention of long distance travel, Brighton and Portsmouth were in different groups as were neighbours Reading and Aldershot!

Group 1 was thought to be a battle between Arsenal and West Ham. Both began on 21 March with wins, the Gunners at White Hart Lane beating Orient 4-1 with Drake scoring twice and West Ham winning 2-1 at Brighton. But the following week the Hammers lost 4-0 at home to Arsenal, the crowd estimated at 19,000. Orient to general surprise had an odd goal in five win over Brighton at Brisbane Road.

Easter Saturday saw Arsenal win 2-1 at Orient while with a George Foreman hat trick West Ham beat Brighton 6-2 at Upton Park. There was a full programme, too on Easter Monday with the Hammers shooting down the Gunners 4-1 at White Hart Lane in front of an 18,405 gathering. Brighton overturned Orient this time 5-2. The following Saturday with Arsenal winning 3-0 at Brighton and West Ham beating Orient 5-3, there was now a two horse race for a group likely to be decided on goal average.

Arsenal had clearly the better such ratio so the Hammers needed to win well but on 18 April Arsenal beat Brighton 5-1 with the help of an own goal a Bastin penalty and two more Lewis goals while West Ham found themselves restricted to a 1-0 win at Orient. So Arsenal booked its semi-final place.

In Group 2 Brentford was the favourite and began impressively beating Aldershot 6-2 at Griffin Park. Millwall and Queen's Park Rangers shared four goals at The Den. A week later Millwall did well to equally divide six goals at Brentford while Aldershot lost 2-0 at home to Rangers. Easter Saturday saw the Lions keeping up the pressure with a 4-2 win at Aldershot while Brentford won the West London affair at Loftus Road against Rangers 2-1. Easter Monday Brentford drew 2-2 at Millwall but Aldershot managed a 2-1 victory at Queen's Park Rangers.

Eddie Perry's second half goal at Griffin Park on 11 April was sufficient for Brentford to overcome Rangers for a total now of eight points. Millwall cracked four against Aldershot at The Den to just one reply and seven points notched up. All rested on 18 April. Brentford made sure of the group winning 3-1 at Aldershot but anyway Millwall had slipped up 2-0 away to Rangers.

Group 3 had the holders Reading expecting keen opposition from Spurs and Charlton, who both made useful starts. Tottenham won 2-1 at Elm Park, Charlton beating Watford 4-1 at Vicarage Road. Spurs followed this beating Watford 5-2 at home while Charlton and Reading drew 1-1 at The Valley though George Tadman missed a penalty for the Addicks. On Easter Saturday Watford caused a surprise winning 1-0 at Charlton while Spurs edged Reading 2-1. Already Spurs looked the most likely winners of the group. Two days later they dropped a point in a goalless draw at Watford as Charlton won 5-3 at Reading where there were hat tricks for both sides: Arsenal's Les Henley for the home team and George Green for Charlton. The Addicks then stunned Spurs on their own patch winning 3-0 and needed just to avoid losing the return at The Valley to finish top. With Grimsby's Fred Kurz scoring four times Watford produced its most comprehensive win of

ORDER FORM

TO: –
SOCCER BOOKS LIMITED
72 ST. PETERS AVENUE,
CLEETHORPES,
N.E. LINCS. DN35 8HU
ENGLAND

FROM ....
....
....
....

PLEASE SEND ME:

TITLE	PRICE £	p	BOOK POSTAGE £	p
TOTAL COST				
-10% Discount (Orders over £60.00)				
Sub Total				
Postage				
I enclose Cheque/Cash/Postal Order **FOR TOTAL**				

I wish to pay by Credit/Debit Card N°   *(cards accepted listed below)*

MasterCard • Visa • American Express • Maestro

Expiry Date .... Start Date (if available) .... Maestro Issue N° ....

Card security code (Last 3 digits on the signature strip or
AmEx: 4 digits printed on card front) ....

E-mail address (please use block capitals):
....

PAL-FORMAT DVDs — COMPLETE MATCHES

Postage for these PAL-format DVDs is charged at **Postage Rate 'A'.**

Discs shown in italics are encoded to Region '2' for use in the UK, Europe, Middle East, South Africa and Japan. DVD players from countries outside of these regions may encounter problems playing Region 2 discs. All other discs are free of region encoding and should play on PAL-format players everywhere.

Note: *The picture quality of many of the earlier games is below the standard of more recent recordings.*

F.A. CUP FINALS   *The price of each of these discs is £13.00 unless otherwise indicated.*

1954 FACF West Brom. v Preston (£16) • 1955 FACF Newcastle v Man. City (£16) • 1957 FACF Aston Villa v Man. United (£16)
1959 FACF Nottingham Forest v Luton Town (£16.00) • 1961 FACF Tottenham Hotspur v Leicester City
1963 FACF Man. United v Leicester City • 1966 FACF Everton v Sheffield Wednesday • 1967 FACF Spurs v Chelsea (Highlights)
1968 West Bromwich Albion v Everton • 1969 FACF Man. City v Leicester City
1970 FACF Chelsea v Leeds United (Full coverage of Replay + First game highlights) • 1971 FACF Arsenal v Liverpool (£20.00)
1974 FACF Liverpool v Newcastle United • 1975 FACF West Ham v Fulham • 1976 FACF Southampton v Man. United (£20)
1977 FACF Man. United v Liverpool • 1979 FACF Arsenal v Manchester United • 1982 FACF Spurs v Queen's Park Rangers
1983 FACF Replay – Man. United v Brighton & Hove Albion • 1984 FACF Everton v Watford • 1985 FACF Man. United v Everton
1986 FACF Liverpool v Everton • 1988 FACF Wimbledon v Liverpool • 1989 FACF Liverpool v Everton
1990 FACF Man. United v Crystal Palace • 1991 FA Cup Semi-Final Spurs v Arsenal • 1991 FACF Spurs v Nottingham Forest
1992 FACF Liverpool v Sunderland • 1993 FACF Arsenal v Sheffield Wednesday • 1994 FACF Man United v Chelsea
1995 FACF Everton v. Man. United • 1996 FACF Manchester United v Liverpool • 1997 FACF Chelsea v Middlesbrough
1998 FACF Arsenal v Newcastle United • 1999 FACF Man. United v Newcastle United • 2002 FACF Arsenal v Chelsea (£18.00)
2006 FACF Liverpool v West Ham (£18) • 2007 FACF Chelsea v Man. United (£16) • 2008 FACF Portsmouth v Cardiff (£16)
2009 FACF Chelsea v Everton (£18) • 2010 FACF Chelsea v Portsmouth (£18) • *2011 FACF Man. City v Stoke (£20.00)*
2012 FACF Chelsea vs Liverpool (£20.00) • 2013 FACF Manchester City vs Wigan Athletic (£25.00) (Includes semi-final)

EUROPEAN CLUB COMPETITION COMPLETE MATCHES

1960 ECF Real Madrid vs Eintracht (£16) • 1963 European Cup-Winners' Cup Final Tottenham Hotspur vs Atletico Madrid (£20)
1965 ECWCF West Ham vs TSV Munich (£16) • 1967 European Cup Final Celtic vs Inter Milan (£16)
1968 European Cup Final Manchester United vs Benfica (£16.00)
1972 UEFA Cup Final Spurs vs Wolverhampton Wanderers (Extended 70 minutes highlights of the First leg only) (£20.00)
1977 EC Final Liverpool vs Borussia Moenchengladbach (£16.00) • 1984 UEFA Cup Final Spurs vs Anderlecht (£16.00)
1985 ECWC Semi-Final Everton 3 Bayern Munich 1 (£13.00)
Liverpool Football Club – 2005 Champions League Final 2005 and The Road to Istanbul (Two programmes on 2 discs) £20.00
Manchester United – Champions League Final 2008 and The Road to Moscow (Two programmes on 2 discs) £23.00
Champions League Final 2009 Barcelona v Man Utd (£20.00) • Champions League Final 2011 Barcelona v Man. United (£20.00)

COMPLETE WORLD CUP MATCHES   *Price of these DVDs is £16.00 unless shown otherwise.*

1962 WC England v Brazil • 1966 WC England v Argentina • 1966 WC England v France • 1966 WC England v Portugal
1966 WC Quarter-Final Portugal v North Korea • *1966 WC Final England v West Germany (Black & White footage)*
1966 WC Brazil v Hungary • 1970 WC Final Brazil vs Italy • 1970 WC England vs Brazil • 1974 WC Final W. Germany vs Holland
1978 WC Final Argentina vs Holland • 1978 WC Scotland v Holland • 1982 WC Brazil v Argentina • 1982 WC Brazil v Italy
1982 WC Final Italy v West Germany • 1986 WC England v Argentina • 1986 WC Final Argentina v West Germany

OTHER WORLD CUP DVDs   *Documentaries featuring highlights and goals. Each priced £16.00.*

FIFA Fever (Includes a new 1930 WC Finals Official Film) • 1950 WC Finals Official Film • 1954 WC Finals Official Film
1958 WC Finals Official Film • 1962 WC Finals Official Film • 1966 WC Finals Official Film • 1970 WC Finals Official Film
1974 WC Finals Official Film • 1978 WC Finals Official Film • 1982 WC Finals Official Film • 1986 WC Finals Official Film
2010 WC Finals Official Film

OTHER MATCHES

1953 England vs Hungary (£16) • 1963 England vs Rest of World (£16) • 1967 England 2 Scotland 3 (Black & White) (£16)
1969 England 4 Scotland 1 (Black & White) (£16.00) • 1967 League Cup Final – Q.P.R. vs West Bromwich (Highlights) (£13)
1991 League Cup Final Sheffield Wednesday vs Man United (£16.00) • 2007 Carling Cup Final Arsenal vs Chelsea (£16.00)
2008 Carling Cup Final Spurs vs Chelsea (£16.00) • Carling Cup Final 2011 – Birmingham City 2 Arsenal 1 (£13.00)
2015 Capital One Cup Final – Chelsea vs Spurs (£18.00) • 2002 Bellissimo! Wales 2 Italy 1 (£10.00)

the season taking six off the fading cup holders Reading.

Charlton duly clinched the group scoring four without reply from Tottenham with the crowd 7,677 at The Valley. Reading managed a face-saving 3-0 win in the turnaround fixture with Watford, but had long since lost their hands on the trophy.

Portsmouth were odds-on to win Group 4 and began confidently enough beating Fulham 9-1. Both Barlow and Steve Griffiths had trebles. However Fulham lost Stan Cullis the Wolves and England captain early in the second half with a broken ankle and collapsed after being just 2-1 down at half-time. There were subsequent repercussions over the rough play in the match. Chelsea and Palace shared six goals at the Bridge. A solitary Conley goal from this Torquay winger won the District Line derby for Fulham against Chelsea though Jackson saved a penalty from Cyril Dean the Cottagers Southampton guest forward while Pompey won 2-0 away to Crystal Palace. In the first of the Easter programme matches Conley shook Pompey with both goals in the Cottagers 2-1 success, the team showing eight changes from the debacle at Fratton Park. Chelsea won 3-0 at Palace. Two days later and another brace for Conley in the 2-2 draw with Chelsea at Stamford Bridge but Pompey edged Crystal Palace 2-1 with a couple from Black.

Fulham had now amazingly emerged as Pompey's only challengers and defeated Crystal Palace 4-1 while another Black brace saw off Chelsea for Portsmouth. But thanks to being thrashed at the outset by Pompey, Fulham's goal average was vastly inferior and only a defeat at Chelsea for Pompey plus Fulham winning at Palace would upset the odds. With a Rooke hat trick Fulham duly came through 4-3 at Palace but Pompey took a point at Stamford Bridge in a goalless draw. A quirk of the match itself was that Portsmouth did not have to take one goal kick throughout the 90 minutes!

On 25 April the first semi-final at Chelsea brought a crowd of 19,036 and a first half goal from Andy Black proved enough for Pompey against Charlton. It took his total of League and Cup goals to 46 for the season. A week on and at the same venue the all-London affair attracted 41,253 with receipts £2,651 in what was a goalless draw between Arsenal and Brentford. The replay was not until 16 May and was held at White Hart Lane which had been Arsenal's "home" ground since the start of the war! It mattered little for Brentford whose pre-war hoodoo over the Gunners carried on. With a first half lead they emerged 2-1 winners after goal from George Wilkins and Doug Hunt, he once of Spurs. With five minutes remaining Brentford's Chelsea goalkeeper Johnny Jackson memorably saved a Bastin penalty. Even the Arsenal response was an own goal by George Poyser. The attendance was 37,600 with takings amounting to £2,700. Extra payments to players were refused the fee was the already standing 30 shillings.

There was considerable Interest in the final between Brentford and Portsmouth at Wembley on 30 May. Admission was three shillings (15p) for the enclosure numbered and reserved seats were variously 30p, 52 and a half pence, 75p and 105p all inclusive of entertainment duty. It resulted in a crowd of 69,792 with receipts £15,000. But it came close to being called off!

Jimmy Guthrie the Portsmouth captain and Players' Union representative had tried unsuccessfully to obtain more money for the players on the occasion of the 1939 FA Cup final against Wolverhampton Wanderers. He adopted more forceful tactics at Wembley in 1942. At 2 p.m. he informed manager Jack Tinn and the club's directors that eight players who had been on Pompey's books at the start of 1939-40 wanted their wages paid for the week ending 9 September 1939 otherwise the team would not play in the final. There were six of them down to play against Brentford.

The stand-off lasted until eight minutes before the kick-off when the directors were forced to give in and agree to the terms. Naturally the crowd had been blissfully unaware of the drama taking place in the dressing-room being entertained with community singing conducted by Arthur Caiger, the man in the white suit.

It proved to be the last battle Guthrie won that day. He had a nightmare of a game, lost out trying to contain Leslie Smith who scored the first goal, fluffed a penalty kick that went straight into Brentford goalkeeper – actually Chelsea's Johnny Jackson's arms – and Smith's second goal glanced in off Guthrie's head! The finalists received £2,500 and all clubs entering received £250 each from the final pool. Though no medals were awarded a bonus of five war savings certificates were donated to the winners and three such for the runners-up. Brentford were worthy 2-0 winners having been runners-up the previous year.

Suffice to say the London League was a success as was its second London Cup, the final at Wembley well attended. Its League competition was well organized under the watchful eye of the London FA and the Football Association with Stanley Rous ever the peacemaker; friend to all and sundry. All fixtures were completed. More importantly for 1942-43 the rebels achieved a higher standing within the Football League after "peace" had been declared and the League South was organized on similar lines to the London League format. Once again George Allison's stature had increased, but misquoting Wellington at Waterloo it had been a "damn close run thing" in view of the threat posed by Guthrie's stance at Wembley.

The aftermath of the Portsmouth-Fulham affair was that Cullis wrote to the FA complaining that the injury had been deliberate. Echoes of the 1939 final when he had played for Wolves against Guthrie as well as most of these players, a theory put forward for the rough treatment meted out to him and other Fulham players. The official response deplored the situation that had arisen but stated there was "insufficient evidence" of any wilful intent. But in May 1942 referees were officially reminded of their duties.

The London War Cup final was not the end of 1941-42. With all clubs now back in the bosom of the Football League, friendly matches were arranged between the London area clubs and those outside. More importantly following a conversation between A V Alexander the First Lord of the Admiralty who was a football man through and through with Chelsea directors had suggested a match for King George's Fund for Sailors. All the necessary authorities agreed and everyone involved donated their services without compensation. So, Wolves who had won the League War Cup final over two legs against Sunderland agreed to meet Brentford in a Cup-Winners' play-off!

It was 6 June 1942, exactly two years before D-Day itself, a blazing hot summer's affair at Stamford Bridge where there were 20,174 present. Eric Robinson the Wolves right-half collapsed just before half-time recovered but succumbed again with 15 minutes remaining diagnosed with a touch of sunstroke! There was no report of the conditions in the press reports or the reason for his malady as weather reporting was forbidden in wartime and these details were only revealed three years later! Sadly Robinson later drowned while engaged on military exercises.

26

Wolves did not of course have the injured Cullis playing, but included four of their 1939 FA Cup side. Brentford had to make one change from the 1942 London Cup final as Tally Sneddon, injured at Wembley, was unfit; Ernie Collett of Arsenal agreed to play providing any souvenir certificates should be handed to Sneddon. This fine gesture was underlined as Collett scored Brentford's equaliser after Jimmy Mullen had opened the scoring for Wolves in the 1-1 draw.

ROUNDING UP THE REST OF DOMESTIC FOOTBALL

Of course, the losers in 1941-42 were the 13 widespread Southern Section clubs with Swansea in the west and Norwich in the east as well as Wolverhampton in the Black Country. Not surprisingly Norwich managed just eight games, Swansea one more. Only Luton Town and Walsall managed to fulfil the 18 games for which the League had hoped. There had been rumours that Norwich might have been able to play games at Ipswich but nothing came of it. With points averaged out for 18 games, Leicester City became the Champions with 26.4 points having played 17 times, narrowly heading West Bromwich Albion who only completed 13 matches for an average of 26.3 points.

The Northern Section's season had been split into regionally based 18 games per club up to Christmas Day with two other competitions following. Blackpool became the League winners by a vastly superior goal average over Lincoln City, though just three points separated the top eight clubs. The League War Cup qualifying competition a two-legged affair began two days later with all available clubs north and south participating except the London League rebels. The intention was for ten ties to be played by each club, the 32 most successful based on a points per game system adjusted to ten matches as not every team managed double figures. Norwich scraped only six games – but still qualified for the cut! From then on it was a knock-out tournament, again over two games but as area conscious as feasible. Oddly enough the Canaries flights away were at Northampton, Luton and Leicester in the qualifying stage and at Northampton, Leicester and Grimsby in the knock-out stage.

There was a snag already in the first round proper first leg designated for the Easter weekend when Blackpool the cup favourites were forced to pull out and give Manchester City a walkover because the War Department forbade service personnel from travelling over the period. Blackpool had ten players in the RAF but goalkeeper Andy Roxburgh was a fireman! At the end of the qualifying competition the 19 unsuccessful clubs were able to play in the Football League Second Championship Series. Of course Blackpool actually made it 20 clubs. Only those managing to play 18 were considered for the Championship itself. Manchester United completed 19 and were declared winners with points adjusted to 23 matches – because Everton was the only club to play as many as 23!

United's points were given as 33.89 – runners-up Blackpool 33.45. However all manner of extra games had been put into the pot. These included ties in the Football League War Cup qualifying competition, knock-out games in the same tournament plus county and regional cup fixtures that bizarrely also counted in some instances as League fixtures! In short, it was a complete shambles to sort out.

Wolves and Sunderland emerged as League War Cup finalists. The two-legged final began at Roker Park and was drawn 2-2 on 23 May watched by 34,776. Wolves won the second leg at Molineux 4-1 in front of 43,038 and took the cup on a 6-3 aggregate.

ODDS AND ENDS FROM THE LONDON LEAGUE AND CUPS

It was understandably a feat for any player to be ever-present in these competitions during 1940-41 and 1941-42. While twelve cup ties in 1940-41 as a maximum if a team reached the final the task was an easier one in 1941-42 it was more difficult. League and Cup commitments totalling 36 without semi-final and final games added for the four teams thus involved made the logistic problems of the time less manageable in finding a full complement of appearances.

Naturally for all clubs siphoned off for these "rebel" competitions, there were more legitimate fixtures under the auspices of the Football League in which they competed, but for the purposes of this particular exercise they were not counted in the overall assessment.

In fact 33 players managed all their club's 1940-41 London Cup ties. Fred Bartlett of Clapton Orient not only achieved it but added an extra guest appearance for Millwall once his club had finished its ties. But it was a much harder in 1941-42 with only five players succeeding in a full list of appearances. They were: Nick Collins (Crystal Palace), Wilf Chitty (Reading), George Foreman (West Ham United) plus the full-back pairing of Sid Tickridge and Ralph Ward at Tottenham Hotspur. Interestingly enough, once Spurs had completed their fixtures, the two helped to complete the Fulham team in its last League game on 23 May against Palace. Tickridge shortly afterwards joined the Royal Navy. Ward, also a useful boxing sparring partner, was a Lieutenant in the Home Guard. Tickridge had been a Millwall guest in 1940-41, too. Chitty and Foreman had appeared in all the London Cup games in 1940-41 to be the only truly ever present performers over the two seasons. Centre-half Bartlett missed only one game in 1941-42 for Orient as did Billy "Buster" Brown the Brentford full-back. Brentford had succeeded in fielding six players in all 1940-41 cup ties, Crystal Palace, Spurs and West Ham four each.

In the 1940-41 London Cup Brentford and Crystal Palace used the fewest players 20 each while Orient had the most with 35. In 1941-42 for League and Cup matches Portsmouth called upon only 29 compared with the 83 utilised by Watford.

As to goal scoring achievements though Foreman with the Hammers had racked up seven and 28 respectively for his tally of 35 over the two seasons, the really big hitters were Reg Lewis at Arsenal and Andy Black of Portsmouth who was their guest from Hearts. Black had 46 goals one more than the Arsenal forward both in 1941-42. But Lewis had the slightly better average as it came from 28 appearances two fewer than Black made. At Fulham, Ronnie Rooke's 40 goals came from ten and 30 respectively having made 34 appearances overall. In fairness it should be added that Jock Dodds with Blackpool played 30 games and scored 65 goals!

There were several other outstanding scoring feats during these two London area campaigns. Leslie Compton at Arsenal appeared in eight London Cup ties in 1940-41 but produced 17 goals including ten against luckless Orient in just one of them. Not a bad return for a once full-back understudy, though in 1941-42 he was seen more in defence.

Everton's Tommy Lawton as an Aldershot guest in 1941-42 had 16 goals in as many games, Jimmy Hagan of Sheffield United playing alongside him at inside-forward scored 15 from his 16 outings. Then in this goals-per-game ratio, the ubiquitous Jock Davie of Brighton showed a fine return for his efforts. For the Seagulls he rattled in 27 goals from 26 games, a hat trick in one of two guest outings at Queen's Park Rangers and one goal in his Reading show for a total of 31 goals in 29 games. Before this in 1940-41 he had scored once in a couple of Brentford appearances and had three goals in as many games for Rangers.

High scoring matches were invariably the result of the absence of a recognised goalkeeper. Despite a motley assortment of outfield players hastily assembled for a particular match at least at some stage there were eleven on one side. There was also an absence of the unfair strictness meted out to Clapton Orient by the Football League when they were trying to scrap together a full complement. There was a war on though perhaps not always appreciated at Preston.

Many players who were able to help out more than just one or two teams were priceless. Top in this particular field was Joe Sibley a Southend United winger whose 27 games in 1941-42 were spread as follows: Fulham 11, Rangers 7, Spurs 3, Millwall 2 plus one each for Aldershot, Chelsea and Palace. Serving in the RAF he must have had a CO with an interest in the game.

Close behind came Eric Jones a winger or inside-forward on the books of West Bromwich Albion. Switched between Brentford and Fulham initially, the odd game at Orient and ended the season as a fairly regular Watford player. Total appearances: 25. Next in the pecking order was Bury's play-anywhere Reg Halton with 23 outings but for just three clubs, four for his Gigg Lane team and also Millwall, the remainder for Aldershot where he was in the Military Police. Sporting all-rounder, too and even started the war delivering letters.

For the highest number of different clubs then Ernie Muttitt of Brentford was the choice. Something of a utility player ideally suited to the demands of the time, he began the season with Fulham, went back to Griffin Park for a game then aided Millwall and Chelsea. Before the season was finished he also wore shirts for Charlton, Palace and Reading. It added up to seven clubs and 22 appearances for the season.

Also on the 22 mark was Sam Malpass actually a Bradford City defender who spasmodically succeeded in playing three times for his own club but eight times for Brighton, seven times for Fulham, twice for Millwall, once for Chelsea and even getting a game for Southampton in that Christmas Day affair when Bristol City turned up with just three of their players, the rest held up in broken down vehicles! He even featured in a Brighton line-up when he was actually playing for Fulham at Portsmouth.

Tommy Kiernan an Albion Rovers inside-forward was a PT instructor in the Royal Engineers and played in Chelsea's first nine 1941-42 games then another five for them. Nearby Fulham was his next call with four in a row followed by three at Spurs in his total of 21. Laurie Kelly another Military Policeman played eleven times for Aldershot, once for Fulham, twice with Brighton and ended the season appearing six times for Orient.

Injuries of course, two of the worst previously mentioned being those affecting Stan Cullis and Leslie Smith. Charlton's Harold Hobbis chipped an ankle bone that kept him sidelined for a time while Joe Payne at Chelsea was taken seriously ill with pneumonia in November 1941 but recovered. The Armed Services, Civil Defence including the Police War Reserve removed most of the available playing talent. For example by 1942 among Arsenal's staff 32 were in the Army, 18 in the RAF, one each in the Royal Navy and Royal Marines. Twenty had originally joined the Territorial Army in the summer of 1939.

As far as attendance figures were concerned, no official information was issued. The national press invariably gave estimated crowds which were invariably inflated from what was likely to be correct. However, Arsenal, Charlton, Portsmouth and Tottenham produced the most accurate returns. Aggregate attendances were probably in excess of one million for the 240 London League matches, with the likelihood of an average gate of at least 4,175 taking the figure to seven digits.

Though the highest figure published was 20,000 for the West Ham v Arsenal match on 24 January at Upton Park, the most accurate was more likely to have been the Arsenal v Spurs affair on 20 September, the Gunners "home match" against their landlords at White Hart Lane returned at 17,446. Arsenal had three other five figure gates and also drew a 15,785 crowd for their visit to Portsmouth on 27 September.

The attraction of Arsenal from their prowess in the 30s remained high and Charlton Athletic's ground produced the Addicks best in 1941-42 with 13,910 inside The Valley for the occasion. A similar story at Brentford (12,000), Brighton (10,000), Chelsea (12,260), Fulham (10,473), Millwall (15,000), Palace (10,024) and Reading (10,000) as the pull of the Reds was widespread. Charlton also recorded the lowest most precise figure with 944 against Brighton on 7 February. A month later the Watford v Crystal Palace match at Vicarage Road, was reported with a congregation as low as 500. In addition at least half a dozen listed variously at 1,000 at Fulham, Orient, Millwall and Watford would have at least matched Charlton's attendance if not in the Watford range.

As with the Football League's own War Cup competition, there were some better crowds for the London Cup especially in 1941-42. Once again the Hammers v Gunners clash was the top at 19,000 but the return at White Hart Lane at 18,405 was more probably higher. Also on 11 April Arsenal attracted an estimated 12,000 to the Goldstone Ground, topping Brighton's previous best of the season also against the Gunners. Chelsea v Fulham in the District Line derby at Stamford Bridge on Easter Monday recorded 10,986 while the same day Portsmouth v Crystal Palace at Fratton Park was watched by 11,671. In the 194041 London Cup the highest crowd had been 9,651 for Spurs v Arsenal on 3 May.

The 1941-42 semi-finals were well supported of course and the 69,792 for the Wembley final between Brentford and Portsmouth was the crowning glory of the rebels' season.

LONDON LEAGUE AND CUP MANAGERS

For managers there was precious little scope for team selection; at times even eleven players would be a bonus. In terms of stature George Allison of Arsenal being the "head honcho" behind the London Cup itself was naturally way above the rest though not in physical terms. His Highbury ground had been requisitioned and was now an ARP fortress. The Gunners lodged with Spurs for football. Having moved his family to Bognor Regis just before the war the area became a restricted military zone and he was forced to decamp to Kingston Hill.

With a journalistic career twinned with leading the 30s most famous club of five Championships and two FA Cup wins following the death of Herbert Chapman he had switched reporting for the *Daily Express* to the *Sunday Chronicle* when the war began. Soon broadcast sporting news to troops in North Africa and even advertised the sale of bicycles on the home front.

During the height of the blitz his property suffered serious damage that rendered it inhabitable and there was also an unexploded landmine in the grounds. He piled young people and four more elderly ones into two cars and they drove to the Arsenal Stadium spending the night in the shelters there. The following day he made arrangements to stay with one of the Reading directors. Allison still commuted to Highbury but it was not a satisfactory situation. However, he was able to have the referees' room at the ground converted into a flat with all the correct amenities. Few others could have pulled that one off in the midst of the blitz. He was also on hand to help with fire watching from the many incendiaries dropped in the vicinity.

He was fortunate that when registered Arsenal players were not at hand, there were always players who would jump at the chance of wearing the red and white shirt. Calls for the many international players with the club meant they were among first choices for representative matches of which there were many organized for charity. Allison had served in the Royal Flying Corps in the Great War.

Another First World War veteran was the Millwall boss Billy Voisey who had enlisted in the Royal Field Artillery reached the rank of Sergeant and won the DCM, MM and the *Croix de Guerre* for conspicuous gallantry. He was attached to the club from his schooldays, scored the club's first Football League goal with a 20 yard drive that earned him the nickname of "Banger." It remained with him throughout life. Played in a Victory International against Wales and toured South Africa with the FA in 1920. Left Millwall in 1923 but came back in 1940 as trainer and manager. Preferred whenever possible to use local youngsters rather than rely on guests but was forced to turn out once at 50. Stationed variously in the locality, many of the players were in the Police War Reserve. Voisey was on hand, too, to act as England attendant for wartime internationals staged at Wembley.

Ted Vizard had won his 22 caps for Wales while with Bolton Wanderers and in a 20 year career with the Trotters played in 467 League games and scored 64 goals from outside-left. After a spell coaching their "A" team he took up an appointment as manager of Swindon Town and in 1939 replaced Billy Birrell as Queen's Park Rangers boss. The Rangers had a sizeable proportion of the playing staff in the Police War Reserve.

As for Peter McWilliam who had two spells leading Tottenham Hotspur initially from 1912 to 1927 and then returning to White Hart Lane in 1938 he had been head hunted earlier but was then acting as a scout for North London rivals Arsenal! He was capped for Scotland the first time in 1905 when a Newcastle United player. League and Cup successes followed him both as a wing-half and manager. Between his two stints at Tottenham he also took the reins at Middlesbrough.

Two managers without any playing experience in the Football League were Harry Curtis at Brentford and Charlie Paynter with West Ham. Curtis may have had limited exposure on the playing side as a youngster with Romford and Walthamstow Grange, but he became a successful referee initially in the Southern League and subsequently at Football League level. But once he became Brentford manager he transformed their fortunes and guided them from the Third Division to the First during the 30s.

Paynter's was a long-serving connection with West Ham dating back to before the turn of the 19th century. He did play for the Hammers but not in the first team and a knee injury ended his career early. With an interest in physiotherapy he became the club's reserve team trainer graduated to the first eleven and in 1932 was appointed manager at Upton Park. Mixed and matched his players 17 of whom were in the Territorial Army at the start of the war, to give everyone a game if possible. Paynter did practically everything at the club and often slept there!

In contrast Jack Peart had a playing career at centre-forward embracing some dozen clubs in and out of the Football League. His appointment as Fulham manager came in the wake of the club dispensing with the services of controversial coach Jimmy Hogan. The directors looked upon Peart as a safe hand on the tiller unlikely to cause any unnecessary waves. He had taken over in 1935 after a brief period in charge under Joe Edelston a former Fulham player of a decade earlier.

Edelston of course had been manager of Reading only from 1939 following a disagreement with the Fulham board when he was running the reserve team there. He took his son Maurice with him to Elm Park. Though qualified as an FA coach thanks to prompting by Hogan, Edelston senior never followed it up. A wing-half he had played for Hull City and Manchester City before linking up with Fulham.

The year 1939 also saw a change at Chelsea with Billy Birrell taking control. He replaced Leslie Knighton. He made a clean sweep of the training staff. Arthur Stollery became trainer, Norman Smith his assistant. Birrell had been an inside-forward with Middlesbrough and skippered the Teeside club, too. He had overcome an injury sustained serving in the Great War and adjusted his style to fit round the slight handicap. At managerial level he had guided Bournemouth and Queen's Park Rangers.

Famous for his off-side trap as a full-back at Newcastle United that led to the law alteration in 1925, Bill McCracken had a managerial career that took in Hull, Gateshead and Millwall whom he left in 1936. His next appointment came a year later at Aldershot where the Home of the British Army afforded him some rare talent for a Third Division club. His Irish charm was able to convince the military of a need to fill his team with the best internationals available, though he always found a place for his own staff wherever possible. He had won 16 caps for Ireland.

Billy Wright at Clapton Orient had an almost impossible task trying to find eleven players each week but performed minor miracles in almost managing it satisfactorily. Twenty-three years at the club from schooldays, a centre-half injured after five years and variously assistant trainer, trainer he had taken over as secretary-manager with the war already underway. He even played in goal when there was no other alternative on hand! Oddly enough Crystal Palace manager George Irwin had also been a goalkeeper in his career including a few years with the Glaziers. He had coached Palace before becoming manager in July 1939. He was fortunate that he had a nucleus of his players in the Civil Defence forces including the Police.

With the expansion to the London League in 1941-42 Charlton Athletic came back into operation and Brighton & Hove Albion, Portsmouth and Watford were recruited. Like Brentford, Charlton had made immense strides from the Third Division into the top flight during the 30s. In May 1933 Jimmy Seed was installed as manager at The Valley after two years in charge of Clapton Orient. The Addicks had finished bottom of the Second Division and relegated. Fifth in 1933-34 they became Third Division (South) Champions in 1934-35, eight points clear of runners-up Reading. They were runners-up again the following season and promoted to the First Division. Amazingly they finished second once more in 1936-37 then a creditable fourth followed by third place in 1938-39. Manager and club seemed admirably suited to each other.

Seed had been an inside-forward briefly with Sunderland and post-Great War with Tottenham Hotspur and Sheffield Wednesday. He was capped five times by England. During the conflict he had served in the 8th Battalion West Yorkshire Regiment and was gassed in France. Not in the best of physical condition Sunderland thought his wartime experiences had ended his career and he was given a free transfer. But Mid Rhondda gave him his second chance and kick-started his playing career.

At Brighton, Charlie Webb was the club's long-serving manager appointed in June 1919 shortly after his release from a German POW camp having been captured in France while serving as an officer in the King's Royal Rifle Corps. From a Scottish military family he was actually born in Ireland and had also served pre-war in the Essex Regiment where he developed as a goal scoring forward. On leave in early 1909 he turned out for Brighton in a Southern League match but as a result was banned from playing for his regiment and the club was fined £5 for including him. He returned to Ireland played for Bohemians in the Irish Cup Final and then signed for the Seagulls as an amateur! Capped by Ireland as an amateur and later three times as a professional while with Brighton he had six years playing for the club. He was its first full international and truly became Mr Brighton & Hove Albion.

Jack Tinn at Portsmouth was another one-off. Appointed manager at Fratton Park in 1927 he inherited a team that had won promotion to the First Division. His predecessor John McCartney had retired through ill-health. Tinn kept Pompey in the top flight though the last two pre-war seasons saw them struggling to stay. He also took them to Wembley three times, initially in 1929 when they lost to Bolton Wanderers then 1934 where they were beaten by Manchester City. It proved third time lucky in 1939 when against all the odds and the hot favourites Wolves they pulled off a sensational 4-1 victory. He gained fame for his superstitions and sporting spats in every round of the cup.

Neil McBain was manager of Watford from 1929 initially combining a player role and gradually improved prospects in the Third Division (South). Though originally an inside-forward he switched to centre-half in an emergency and found his true position. A Scot he swapped trade as a carpenter and joiner for football, served in both the Army and Navy during the Great War. From Hamilton Academicals and Ayr United he graduated post-war to Manchester United, Everton, St Johnstone and Liverpool, winning three full caps for Scotland along the way.

While gradual improvement was noticeable on the field, problems concerning his dealings off the pitch with the board and players led to McBain being replaced by another player Bill Findlay for 1937-38. Watford had finished sixth, fifth and fourth in successive seasons. They stayed fourth for the next two terms. Come wartime football and Findlay had to dust off his boots to help out when the need arose. Also a Scot, he had previously played for Third Lanark, Liverpool and Leicester City.

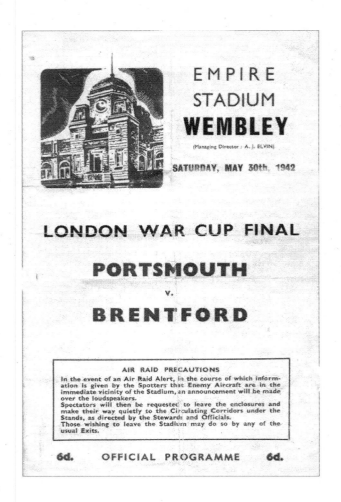

Programme and 2/- standing ticket for the 1942 London War Cup Final at Wembley Stadium.

ARSENAL FOOTBALL CLUB, LTD.
OFFICIAL PROGRAMME.

NOVEMBER 1st, 1941.   Price:—ONE PENNY.

LONDON WAR LEAGUE.	LONDON WAR LEAGUE.
On Saturday, November 8th—	On Saturday, November 15th—
SPURS v. CLAPTON ORIENT	**ARSENAL v. CLAPTON ORIENT**
Kick-off 3 p.m.	Kick-off 3 p.m.

London War League   Sat., Nov., 1st, 1941.   Kick-off 3.0 p.m.

ARSENAL 3

Red Shirts, White Sleeves and Collars; Knickers White; Stockings Blue, White Rings and White Tops.

RIGHT WING.   LEFT WING.

1
Marks
Goal

2   3
Male   Compton, L. (CAPt)
Right Back   Left Back

4   5   6
Crayston   Collett   Jones, L.
Right Half   Centre Half   Left Half

7   MILLER, I.   9   10   11
Cumner   Blakeney   Lewis   Bastin   Compton, D.
Outside Right   Inside Right   Centre   Inside Left   Outside Left

Referee—Mr. R. C. GREENWOOD

Linesmen—Mr. R. R. MAY (Blue and White Flag).
Mr. T. BOWYER (Red and White Flag).

11   10   9   8   7
Halton   Blair   Lawton   Hagan   Raynor
Outside Left   Inside Left   Centre   Inside Right   Outside Right
                (CAPt).

6   5   4
Taylor   Walters   Britton
Left Half   Centre Half   Right Half

3   2
Jefferson   Sheppard
Left Back   Right Back

1
Putt
Goal

LEFT WING.   RIGHT WING.

ALDERSHOT 2.

Blue shirts, Blue sleeves, stockings, White collars cuffs,

ANY ALTERATION WILL BE NOTED ON THE BOARD.

AIR RAID SHELTER.

In the event of an Air Raid Warning being received, the Police will instruct the Referee to stop the game when they deem it necessary and the players will leave the field. Spectators must take shelter and remain under cover until the "All Clear" has been given.

Will patrons please refrain from changing their positions and going from behind one Goal to the other.

Programme for the Arsenal v Aldershot game on November 1st 1941. Arsenal's home games were played at White Hart Lane since Highbury suffered bomb damage and was used for the war effort.

GAMES, RESULTS, SCORERS

LONDON CUP 1940-41 GROUP A

4 January 1941
Aldershot (0) 1 Chelsea (0) 0, Recreation Ground, 2000. Scorer: Brooks.
Brentford (2) 2 Crystal Palace (1) 2, Griffin Park,1000. Scorers: Muttitt, Boulter; Dawes A 2.
Fulham (2) 4 Queen's Park Rangers (1) 1, Craven Cottage, 1000. Scorers: Revell, Swinfen (og), Rooke, Keeping; Mangnall.

11 January 1941
Chelsea (3) 5 Aldershot (0) 1, Stamford Bridge, 2000. Scorers: Spence 2, Hurley, Kurz, Galloway; Bamford.
Crystal Palace (1) 2 Brentford (2) 2, Selhurst Park, 2841. Scorers: Dawes A, Robson; Muttitt, Smith.
Queen's Park Rangers (3) 5 Fulham (1) 7, Loftus Road, 2256. Scorers: Lowe, March, Bonass, Bott, Mangnall; Rooke 4, Woodward, Evans, Robinson.

25 January 1941
Chelsea (0) 0 Brentford (0) 1, Stamford Bridge, 1318. Scorer: Hunt.
Crystal Palace (2) 5 Fulham (0) 2, Selhurst Park, 2000. Scorers: Dawes A 3, Robson, Smith; Revell, Beasley.
Queen's Park Rangers (2) 2 Aldershot (0) 3, Loftus Road, 1000. Scorers: Mallett 2; Britton, Bamford, Ray.

1 February 1941
Aldershot (2) 3 Crystal Palace (3) 3, Recreation Ground, 2000. Scorers: Brooks, Hagan, Raynor; Smith, Blackman, Robson.
Fulham (3) 4 Brentford (0) 1, Craven Cottage, 2400. Scorers: Revell, Rooke, Beasley, O'Callaghan; Smith.
Queen's Park Rangers (2) 5 Chelsea (1) 2, Loftus Road, 1900.
Scorers: Lowe, Mangnall, McEwan 2, Bott; Tennant, Galloway.

8 February 1941
Aldershot (1) 2 Queen's Park Rangers (2) 4, Recreation Ground, 2000. Scorers: Hagan 2; Mangnall, Daniels, Adam, March.
Brentford (4) 7 Fulham (1) 4, Griffin Park, 2000. Scorers: McKenzie, Hunt, Hopkins 3, Perry 2; O'Callaghan 2, Keeping, Smith.
Crystal Palace (0) 3 Chelsea (1) 3, Selhurst Park, 3703. Scorers: Blackman, Robson, Dawes A; Galloway, Spence, Kurz.

1 March 1941
Fulham (0) 1 Crystal Palace (1) 4, Craven Cottage, 2500. Scorers: Robinson; Robson 4.

15 March 1941
Aldershot (2) 3 Fulham (1) 1, Recreation Ground, 2500. Scorers: Dawes A 2, Morgan; Trewick.

22 March 1941
Aldershot (1) 4 Fulham (1) 1, Recreation Ground, 3000. Scorers: Bamford 2, Chalmers, Dawes A;
Rooke, Cullis
(Both matches at Aldershot).

29 March 1941
Brentford (1) 2 Chelsea (1) 2, Griffin Park, 1654. Scorers: Smith, Townsend; Kiernan 2.

5 April 1941
Brentford (1) 4 Aldershot (0) 2, Griffin Park, 1960. Scorers: Perry 2, Hopkins 2;
Gallacher, Bamford.
Chelsea (1) 1 Crystal Palace (2) 3, Stamford Bridge, 3500. Scorers: Kurz; Wilson A 2, Robson.

12 April 1941
Aldershot (0) 2 Brentford (0) 2, Recreation Ground, 4000. Scorers: Raynor, Hagan;
Wilkins, Perry.
Crystal Palace (0) 1 Queen's Park Rangers (0) 2, Selhurst Park, 5000. Scorers: Blackman;
Mangnall, Fitzgerald.
Fulham (1) 4 Chelsea (0) 0, Craven Cottage, 5000. Scorers: Woodward 2, Rooke, O'Callaghan.

14 April 1941
Brentford (1) 4 Queen's Park Rangers (2) 2, Griffin Park, 5000. Scorers: Hopkins, Perry 2, Smith;
Mangnall 2.
Crystal Palace (0) 1 Aldershot (0) 0, Selhurst Park, 2000. Scorer: Robson.

19 April 1941
Chelsea (1) 4 Fulham (2) 3, Stamford Bridge, 2712. Scorers: Malpass (og), Kurz 2, Mills;
Rooke 2, Woodward.
Queen's Park Rangers (2) 2 Crystal Palace (0) 1, Loftus Road, 2000. Scorers: Davie 2; Robson.

26 April 1941
Queen's Park Rangers (0) 0 Brentford (0) 0, Loftus Road, 6000.

3 May 1941
Chelsea (0) 2 Queen's Park Rangers (1) 3, Stamford Bridge, 4000. Scorers: Spence 2;
Mangnall 2, Davie.

LONDON CUP 1940-41 GROUP B

4 January 1941
Millwall (1) 1 West Ham United (1) 2, The Den, 2500. Scorers: Jinks; Foreman, Goulden.
Reading (0) 2 Arsenal (0) 0, Elm Park, 6158. Scorers: Edelston, MacPhee.
Tottenham Hotspur (2) 3 Clapton Orient (0) 0, White Hart Lane, 1513. Scorer: Gibbons 3.

11 January 1941
Arsenal (0) 0 Reading (1) 1, White Hart Lane, 3069. Scorer: Cothliff.
Clapton Orient (0) 1 Tottenham Hotspur (2) 9, Brisbane Road, 1013. Scorers: Fletcher C;
Hall, Duncan, Gibbons 3, Broadis 2, Ludford 2.
West Ham United (1) 2 Millwall (1) 1, Upton Park, 3500. Scorers: Foreman, Hobbis; Fisher.

18 January 1941
Millwall (1) 1 Tottenham Hotspur (1) 3, The Den, 6000. Scorers: Forsyth;
Gibbons 2, Broadis.

25 January 1941
Clapton Orient (0) 0 Reading (3) 4, Brisbane Road, 300. Scorers: Cothliff, Edelston 2, MacPhee.
Tottenham Hotspur (0) 4 Millwall (0) 0, White Hart Lane, 2280. Scorers: Ward, Broadis, Ludford 2.
West Ham United (0) 1 Arsenal (1) 3, Upton Park, 5000. Scorers: Bicknell; Drake, Curtis, Bastin.

1 February 1941
Clapton Orient (1) 3 Arsenal (1) 3, Brisbane Road, 1200. Scorers: McNeil 3;
Compton L, Kirchen, Bastin.
Millwall (0) 0 Reading (1) 2, The Den, 1300. Scorers: Brooks, MacPhee.
Tottenham Hotspur (0) 1 West Ham United (0) 2, White Hart Lane, 4691. Scorers: Broadis;
Small, Fenton.

8 February 1941
Arsenal (4) 15 Clapton Orient (0) 2, White Hart Lane, 2780. Scorers: Compton L 10, Bastin 2,
Jones L, Compton D 2; Rawlings, McNeil.
Reading (2) 2 Millwall (0) 2, Elm Park, 4592. Scorers: Layton (pen), Shrwood; Jinks, Dudley.
West Ham United (1) 3 Tottenham Hotspur (1) 2, Upton Park, 5200. Scorers: Foreman, Small,
Foxall; Gibbons, Hall.

1 March 1941
Clapton Orient (0) 0 Millwall (0) 1, Brisbane Road, 350. Scorer: Reid.

22 March 1941
Millwall (0) 1 Arsenal (2) 6, The Den, 5500. Scorers: Fisher;
Nelson, Crayston, Henley, Compton L 3.
West Ham United (0) 1 Reading (0) 1, Upton Park, 2533. Scorers: Hobbis; MacPhee.

29 March 1941
Reading (6) 9 Clapton Orient (0) 0, Elm Park, 3000. Scorers: MacPhee 4, Deverall, Bradley 2,
Chitty, Brooks.

5 April 1941
Millwall (2) 4 Clapton Orient (0) 0, The Den, 1500. Scorers: Reeve 3, Johnson.
Reading (1) 4 West Ham United (1) 1, Elm Park, 5000. Scorers: Layton, Cothliff, MacPhee 2.

12 April 1941
West Ham United (4) 8 Clapton Orient (0) 1, Upton Park, 2800. Scorers: Small 2, Foxall, Corbett,
Goulden, Foreman 2, Chalkley.

14 April 1941
Tottenham Hotspur (0) 2 Reading (2) 2, White Hart Lane, 4355. Scorers: Wallace, Duncan;
MacPhee, Chitty.

19 April 1941
Clapton Orient (1) 2 West Ham United (1) 3, Brisbane Road, 1000. Scorers: Fisher, Fletcher C;
Foreman 2, Small.
Reading (0) 2 Tottenham Hotspur (1) 2, Elm Park, 5500. Scorers: MacPhee, Layton;
Duncan, Ludford.

3 May 1941
Tottenham Hotspur (1) 3 Arsenal (1) 3, White Hart Lane, 9651. Scorers: Bennett K, Ward, Gibbons;
Compton L 2, Kirchen.

17 May 1941
Arsenal (0) 3 West Ham United (0) 0, White Hart Lane, 7365. Scorers: Drake 2, Compton L (pen).

21 May 1941
Arsenal (0) 0 Tottenham Hotspur (2) 3, White Hart Lane, 6673. Scorers: Duncan 2, Gibbons.

24 May 1941
Millwall (1) 2 Arsenal (1) 5, The Den, 5000. Scorers: Osborne J, Reid;
Drake 3, Henley, Blakeney.
(Both matches at Millwall).

31 May 1941
Semi-finals:
Reading (3) 4 Crystal Palace (1) 1, Elm Park, 5303. Scorers: MacPhee 3, Edelston; Blackman.
Tottenham Hotspur (0) 0 Brentford (0) 2, White Hart Lane, 6495. Scorers: Perry, Townsend.

7 June 1941
Final:
Reading (1) 3 Brentford (1) 2, Stamford Bridge, 9000.
Scorers: Sherwood, Chitty, Edelston; Perry 2.

LONDON LEAGUE 1941-42

30 August 1941
Brentford (1) 4, Arsenal (1) 1, Griffin Park, 12,000. Scorers: Hapgood (og), Wilkins, Smith, Perry; Nelson.
Brighton & Hove Albion (1) 2, Queen's Park Rangers (2) 5, Goldstone Ground, 3000.
Scorers: Shafto, Balmer; Mahon, Davie 3, Paterson.
Charlton Athletic (2) 2, Chelsea (1) 1, The Valley, 6793. Scorers: Welsh 2; Spence.
Clapton Orient (1) 3, Reading (4) 8, Brisbane Road, 2000. Scorers: Armstrong 2, Fletcher; Edelston 3, Bradley 2, Sherwood 1, MacPhee, Chitty.
Crystal Palace (0) 2, Millwall (0) 0, Selhurst Park, 4764. Scorers: Robson, Gillespie.
Fulham (1) 2, Aldershot (2) 6, Craven Cottage, 3500. Scorers: Rooke 2 (1 pen);
Lawton 2, Hagan 2, Glasby, Taylor.
Tottenham Hotspur (2) 5, Watford (0) 0, White Hart Lane, 5074. Scorers: Ludford 3, Gibbons 2.
West Ham United (1) 1, Portsmouth (0) 3, Upton Park, 6250. Scorers: Foxall; Black 2, Barlow.

6 September 1941
Aldershot (1) 3, Tottenham Hotspur (1) 2, Recreation Ground, 5000. Scorers: Palmer, Britton, Lawton; Gibbons 2.
Arsenal (4) 7, Crystal Palace (1) 2, White Hart Lane, 6207. Scorers: Lewis 5, Bastin 2;
Hawke, Robson.
Charlton Athletic (3) 4, Clapton Orient (0) 0, The Valley, 3565. Scorers: Revell, Dryden, Tadman 2.
Chelsea (2) 4, West Ham United (2) 8, Stamford Bridge, 6427. Scorers: Payne, Smith C, Kurz, Kiernan; Foreman 3, Foxall 2, Small, Fenton, Goulden.
Millwall (0) 2, Fulham (1) 4, The Den, 5000. Scorers: Richardson, Smith J R;
Muttitt, Cranfield, Rooke 2.
Queen's Park Rangers (1) 3, Brentford (3) 4, Loftus Road, 8000. Scorers: Mallett, Halford, Mahon;
Perry 2, Hunt, Wilkins.
Reading (1) 4, Brighton & Hove Albion (2) 5, Elm Park, 4041. Scorers: MacPhee 2, Chitty, Cothliff; Balmer 2, Pearson, Taylor, Tunnicliffe.
Watford (0) 1, Portsmouth (1) 5, Vicarage Road, 3691. Scorers: Galley; Barlow 3, Black 2.

13 September 1941
Brentford (1) 3, Reading (1) 2, Griffin Park, 6100. Scorers: Perry 2, Wilkins; Deverall 2.
Charlton Athletic (1) 1, West Ham United (1) 1, The Valley, 7673. Scorers: Revell; Foreman.
Clapton Orient (1) 3, Brighton & Hove Albion (1) 3, Brisbane Road, 2000. Scorers: Crawford, Willshaw 2; Davie 2, Easdale.
Crystal Palace (0) 2, Queen's Park Rangers (1) 1, Selhurst Park, 4500. Scorers: Robson, Dawes A; Halford.
Fulham (0) 2, Arsenal (3) 5 Craven Cottage, 10,473. Scorers: Cranfield, Rooke; Lewis 3, Henley, Kirchen.
Portsmouth (0) 2, Aldershot (0) 2, Fratton Park, 6328. Scorers: Black, Parker; Neill, Halton (pen).
Match abandoned 77 minutes; broken goal post; result stood.
Tottenham Hotspur (2) 3, Millwall (0) 0, White Hart Lane, 6656. Scorers: Bennett, Gibbons, Ludford.
Watford (1) 1, Chelsea (0) 3, Vicarage Road, 4000. Scorers: Biggs; Payne, Kurz, Spence.

20 September 1941

Arsenal (1) 4, Tottenham Hotspur (0) 0, White Hart Lane, 17,446 Scorers: Cumner 2, Lewis 2.

Brighton & Hove Albion (0) 2, Brentford (1) 2, Goldstone Ground, 5000. Scorers: Wilson, Balmer; Perry, Hunt.

Charlton Athletic (2) 5, Watford (1) 1, The Valley, 3663. Scorers::Hobbis 2, Green, Baxter, Revell; Biggs.

Chelsea (3) 4, Aldershot (0) 0, Stamford Bridge, 6000. Scorers: Galloway 2, Smith J 2.

Millwall (0) 1, Portsmouth (1) 3, The Den, 3507. Scorers: Smith J R; Black 2, Moores.

Queen's Park Rangers (1) 2, Fulham (3) 5, Loftus Road, 5500. Scorers: Eastham 2; Sibley, Rooke 4.

Reading (4) 6, Crystal Palace (1) 2, Elm Park, 4000. Scorers: MacPhee 5, Chitty; Robson, Blackman.

West Ham United (2) 3, Clapton Orient (0) 1, Upton Park, 4500. Scorers: Macaulay, Foreman, Foxall; Willshaw.

27 September 1941

Aldershot (1) 1, Charlton Athletic (0) 0, 5316. Scorer: Hagan.

Brighton & Hove Albion (1) 2, Crystal Palace (1) 2, Goldstone Ground, 4000. Scorers: Balmer, Ramsden; Hudgell (pen), Robson.

Clapton Orient (1) 1, Brentford (1) 3, Brisbane Road, 3500. Scorers: Fletcher; Perry, Smith, Hopkins.

Fulham (2) 2, Reading (1) 2, Craven Cottage, 6019. Scorers: Rooke 2; Edelston, MacPhee.

Millwall (4) 6, Chelsea (2) 3, The Den, 5500. Scorers: Reid 2, Bell, Fisher, Smith J R, own goal; Galloway 3.

Portsmouth (0) 1, Arsenal (1) 5, Fratton Park, 15,785. Scorers: Guthrie; Bastin 2, Lewis 2, Henley.

Tottenham Hotspur (2) 3, Queen's Park Rangers (0) 1, White Hart Lane, 5955. Scorers: Ludford 2, Noble; Mangnall.

Watford (0) 0, West Ham United (1) 8, Vicarage Road, 4000. Scorers: Foreman 3, Foxall 2, Nieuwenhuys 2, Small.

4 October 1941

Arsenal (2) 3, Chelsea (0) 0, White Hart Lane, 7747. Scorers: Lewis, Crayston, Weaver (og).

Brentford (1) 1, Crystal Palace (0) 2, Griffin Park, 4700. Scorers: Perry; Blackman, Smith T.

Charlton Athletic (1) 1, Millwall (1) 2, The Valley, 5797. Scorers: Revell; Reid (pen), Bell.

Fulham (1) 2, Brighton & Hove Albion (3) 3, Craven Cottage, 2500. Scorers: Morgan, McCormick; Stephens 2, Davie.

Queen's Park Rangers (0) 0, Portsmouth (1) 2, Loftus Road, 2935. Scorer: Black 2.

Reading (1) 1, Tottenham Hotspur (1) 1, Elm Park, 5484. Scorers: Bradley; Gibbons.

Watford (0) 2, Clapton Orient (2) 2, Vicarage Road, 2000 Scorers: Waller, Galley; Bestwick, Willshaw.

West Ham United (1) 3, Aldershot (0) 0, Upton Park, 5500. Scorers: Foreman 2, Barrett (pen).

11 October 1941

Aldershot (5) 8, Watford (1) 1, Recreation Ground, 3000. Scorers: Lawton 3, Hagan 2, Halton, Raynor, Britton; Briggs.

Charlton Athletic (0) 1, Arsenal (2) 3, The Valley, 13,910. Scorers: Welsh; Lewis, Bastin, Crayston.

Crystal Palace (0) 2, Clapton Orient (0) 0, Selhurst Park, 3400. Scorers: Wilson, Dawes A.

Fulham (1) 4, Brentford (0) 3, Craven Cottage, 6000 Scorers: Gallacher 2, Hiles 2; Townsend, Smailes, Perry.

Portsmouth (1) 1, Reading (0) 0, Fratton Park, 5441. Scorer: Moores.

Queen's Park Rangers (0) 2, Chelsea (1) 1, Loftus Road, 6000. Scorers: Mahon, Mallett; Kurz.

Tottenham Hotspur (0) 1, Brighton & Hove Albion (1) 2, White Hart Lane, 4542. Scorers: Broadis; Balmer 2.

West Ham United (3) 4, Millwall (2) 2, Upton Park, 7500. Scorers: Foreman 2, Nieuwenhuys, Bicknell; Bell 2.

18 October 1941

Aldershot (1) 1, Clapton Orient (1) 1, Recreation Ground, 2500. Scorers: Halton; Crawford.

Arsenal (3) 4, West Ham United (0) 1, White Hart Lane, 13,419. Scorers: Lewis 2, Kirchen, Compton D; Foreman.

Brentford (1) 1, Tottenham Hotspur (1) 4, Griffin Park, 6000. Scorers: Hunt; Noble, Duncan 2, Ludford.

Brighton & Hove Albion (0) 2, Portsmouth, (1) 1, Goldstone Ground, 4250. Scorers: Jones, Tunnicliffe; McIntosh.

Chelsea (0) 0, Reading (0) 5, Stamford Bridge, 2945. Scorers: Edelston 3, MacPhee, Bradley.

Crystal Palace (2) 3, Fulham (0) 1, Selhurst Park, 5000. Scorers: Robson 2, Barke; Hiles.

Millwall (2) 4, Watford (2) 2, The Den, 2500. Scorers: Fisher 3, Lawton; Westcott 2.

Queen's Park Rangers (0) 0, Charlton Ath (0) 0, Loftus Road, 5500.

25 October 1941

Aldershot (0) 5, Millwall (0) 2, Recreation Ground, 3000. Scorers: Halton 3, Raynor, Mahon; Osborne, Fisher.

Charlton Athletic (2) 2, Reading (1) 3, The Valley, 3288. Scorers: Hobbis, Tadman; Bradley 2 (1 pen), MacPhee.

Chelsea (0) 1, Brighton & Hove Albion (0) 3, Stamford Bridge, 3000. Scorers: Galloway; Davie 3.

Clapton Orient (0) 2, Fulham (1) 1, Brisbane Road, 2000. Scorers: Willshaw 2; Jones E.

Portsmouth (1) 2, Brentford (0) 1, Fratton Park, 5806. Scorers: Parker, Rochford; Hunt.

Tottenham Hotspur (0) 1, Crystal Palace (1) 1, White Hart Lane, 4807. Scorers: Ludford; Robson.

Watford (1) 3, Arsenal (0) 1, Vicarage Road, 6000. Scorers: Jones T, Kilhourhy, Morris; Beasley.

West Ham United (0) 2, Queen's Park Rangers (0) 0, 5300. Scorers: Macaulay, Foreman.

1 November 1941

Arsenal (2) 3, Aldershot (0) 2, White Hart Lane, 8884. Scorers: Miller, Lewis, Compton D; Blair, Raynor.

Brentford (1) 3, Chelsea (0) 1, Griffin Park, 6000. Scorers: Perry, James, Hunt; Tennant.

Brighton & HA (1) 3, Charlton Athletic (3) 5, Goldstone Ground, 4800. Scorers: Davie 2, Hart; Green 2, Whittaker, Smith, Welsh.

Crystal Palace (1) 3, Portsmouth (1) 1, Selhurst Park, 5493. Scorers: Robson 2, Collins; Black.

Fulham (2) 2, Tottenham Hotspur (1) 2, Craven Cottage, 6000. Scorers: Rooke 2; Noble, Gibbons.

Millwall (1) 2, Clapton Orient (0) 2, The Den, 2000. Scorers: Osborne 2; Willshaw 2.

Queen's Park Rangers (0) 1, Watford (2) 5, Loftus Road, 3000. Scorers: Pattison; Westcott 5.

Reading (1) 3, West Ham United (1) 2, Elm Park, 6000. Scorers: Cothliff 2, Chitty; Bicknell, Macaulay.

8 November 1941

Aldershot (1) 4, Queen's Park Rangers (0) 1, Recreation Ground, 4000. Scorers: Lawton 4; Pattison (pen).

Brentford (1) 2, Charlton Athletic (1) 1, Griffin Park, 6320. Scorers: Smith, Hunt; Dryden.

Chelsea (1) 1, Crystal Palace (0) 0, Stamford Bridge, 3000. Scorer: Wrigglesworth.

Millwall (0) 2, Arsenal (2) 2, The Den, 15,000. Scorers: Fisher, Bell; Miller, Male.

Portsmouth (3) 5, Fulham (1) 3, Fratton Park, 6324. Scorers: Black 2, Ward 2, Parker; Gallacher, Rooke, Richardson.

Tottenham Hotspur (0) 2, Clapton Orient (0) 0, White Hart Lane, 5685. Scorers: Broadis, Gibbons.

Watford (0) 0, Reading (0) 0, Vicarage Road, 4370.

West Ham United (0) 4, Brighton & Hove Albion, Upton Park, 5600. Scorers: Foreman 2, Goulden 2.

15 November 1941

Arsenal (3) 5, Clapton Orient (0) 2, White Hart Lane, 7036. Scorers: Lewis 3, Compton L 2; Armstrong 2.

Brentford (0) 0, West Ham United (1) 5, Griffin Park, 5000. Scorers: Foxall 2, Small 2, Goulden.

Brighton & Hove Albion (1) 2, Watford (0) 2, Goldstone Ground, 4000. Scorers: Davie, Cunliffe; Robinson T, Broome.

Crystal Palace (2) 4, Charlton Athletic (0) 0, Selhurst Park, 5300. Scorers: Gillespie 2, Robson 2.

Fulham (0) 1, Chelsea (2) 4, Craven Cottage, 4994. Scorers: Freeman; Smith JF 2, Galloway, Weale.

Portsmouth (1) 1, Tottenham Horspur (0) 2, Fratton Park, 6044. Scorers: Black; Ludford, Broadis.

Queen's Park Rangers (1) 4, Millwall (0) 1, 3500. Scorers: Stock 2, Mahon, Pattison; Bell.

Reading (3) 3, Aldershot (2) 3, Elm Park, 6000. Scorers: Chitty 2, MacPhee; Hagan, Lawton, Blair.

22 November 1941

Aldershot (2) 5, Brighton & Hove Albion (0) 1, Recreation Ground, 3000. Scorers: Blair 2, Ray, Jones, Campbell; Hart.

Arsenal (1) 4, Queen's Park Rangers (0) 1, White Hart Lane, 7377. Scorers: Miller 2, Compton D 2; Pattison.

Charlton Athletic (2) 3, Fulham (2) 3, The Valley, 3091. Scorers: Lancelotte, Ford, Welsh; Rooke 2 (1 pen), Gallacher.

Chelsea (0) 1, Tottenham Hotspur (0) 1, Stamford Bridge, 6718. Scorers: Galloway; Duncan.

Clapton Orient (0) 0, Portsmouth (2) 4, Brisbane Road, 2403. Scorers: Moores, Ward, Aston, Barnes (og).

Reading (1) 2, Millwall (1) 1, Elm Park, 4200. Scorers: MacPhee, Beasley; Bell.

Watford (1) 1, Brentford (2) 6, Vicarage Road, 4000. Scorers: Kilhourhy; Perry 4, Hopkins 2.

West Ham United (0) 0 Crystal Palace (1) 5, Upton Park, 7000. Scorers: Barke 2, Blackman, Gillespie, Robson.

29 November 1941

Arsenal (2) 3, Reading (0) 1, White Hart Lane, 8198. Scorers: Lewis 2, Miller; MacPhee.

Brentford (0) 5, Aldershot (0) 1, Griffin Park, 4410. Scorers: Hunt 2, Hopkins, Townsend, Duns; Britton.

Brighton & Hove Albion (2) 5, Millwall (0) 0, Goldstone Ground, 3000. Scorers: Davie 2, Cunliffe 2, Wilson.

Charlton Athletic (0) 2, Tottenham Hotspur (0) 1, The Valley, 4210. Scorers: Lancelotte, Welsh; Ludford.

Clapton Orient (0) 0, Queen's Park Rangers (0) 0, Brisbane Road, 2000.

Crystal Palace (2) 6, Watford (1) 1, Selhurst Park, 4000. Scorers: Barke 2, Dawes A, Gillespie, Blackman, Wilson; Lewis G.

Fulham (0) 1, West Ham United (3) 3, Craven Cottage, 4468. Scorers: Jones L; Small 2, Goulden.

Portsmouth (0) 2, Chelsea (0) 3, Fratton Park, 6469. Scorers: Moores, Black; Weaver, Weale, Smith JF.

6 December 1941

Aldershot (1) 1, Crystal Palace (2) 2, Recreation Ground, 2000. Scorers: Ray; Collins, Robson.

Brighton & Hove Albion (1) 2, Arsenal (1) 3, Goldstone Ground, 10,000. Scorers: Davie, Wilson; Bastin (pen), Drake, Miller.

Chelsea (1) 1, Clapton Orient (0) 3, Stamford Bridge, 2718. Scorers: Galloway; Willshaw, Odell, Armstrong.

Millwall (2) 4, Brentford (2) 2, The Den, 2000. Scorers: Osborne 2, Bell, Mansfield; Muttitt, Townsend.

Portsmouth (5) 7, Charlton Athletic (0) 2, Fratton Park, 4336. Scorers: Black 4, Griffiths 2, Barlow; Gibbs, Mason.

Reading (1) 2, Queen's Park Rangers (0) 2, Elm Park, 3177. Scorers: MacPhee, Taylor; Armstrong, Kirkham.

Tottenham Hotspur (0) 1, West Ham United (1) 1, White Hart Lane, 8493. Scorers: Broadis; Foxall.

Watford (0) 3, Fulham (1) 5, Vicarage Road, 1000. Scorers: Cringan, Lewis H, Barnett; Conley 2, Gallacher 2, Thomas.

13 December 1941

Aldershot (4) 4, Fulham (0) 3, Recreation Ground, 3000. Scorers: Geldard 3, Lawton; Rooke 2 (1 pen), Rampling.

Arsenal (0) 1, Brentford (2) 3, White Hart Lane, 9739. Scorers: Crayston; Smith, Duns, Perry.

Chelsea (1) 2, Charlton Athletic (3) 4, Stamford Bridge, 3500. Scorers: Spence, Weale; Welsh 2, Hobbis, Salmond (og).

Millwall (1) 1, Crystal Palace (0) 0, The Den, 5100. Scorer: Wright.

Portsmouth (0) 1, West Ham United (0) 0, Fratton Park, 6319. Scorer: Black.

Queen's Park Rangers (3) 3, Brighton & Hove Albion (0) 0, Loftus Road, 3000. Scorers: Mangnall 2, Armstrong.

Reading (2) 2, Clapton Orient (0) 0, Elm Park, 2809. Scorers: Edelston 2.

Watford (0) 1, Tottenham Hotspur (1) 2, Vicarage Road, 3000. Scorers: Egan; Hall GW, White.

20 December 1941

Brentford (2) 4, Queen's Park Rangers (0) 3, Griffin Park, 3500. Scorers: Townsend 3, Hunt; Mangnall 2, Abel.

Brighton & Hove Albion (1) 1, Reading (2) 5, Goldstone Ground, 2400. Scorers: Wilson; Edelston 3, MacPhee, Chitty.

Clapton Orient (0) 1, Charlton Athletic (1) 1, Brisbane Road, 1000. Scorers: Tully; Welsh. *Match abandoned 57 minutes, due to fog; result stood.*

Fulham (3) 4, Millwall (0) 3, Craven Cottage, 1000. Scorers: Rooke 4; Bell, Osborne, Wright.

Portsmouth (3) 7, Watford (1) 1, Fratton Park, 4633. Scorers: Black 3, Barlow 2, Griffiths 2 (1 pen); Griffiths (pen).

Tottenham Hotspur (0) 1, Aldershot (1) 1, White Hart Lane, 4250. Scorers: White; Raynor.

West Ham United (3) 5, Chelsea (0) 0, Upton Park, 3800. Scorers: Foreman, Fenton, Goulden, Foxall, Macaulay.

Crystal Palace v Arsenal postponed.

25 December 1941

Aldershot (2) 3, Portsmouth (0) 2, Recreation Ground, 4715. Scorers: Raynor, Hunt, Glasby; Emery, Guthrie (pen).

Arsenal (0) 2, Fulham (0) 0, White Hart Lane, 10,578. Scorers: Lewis, Kirchen.

Brighton & HA (2) 4, Clapton Orient (1) 1, Goldstone Ground, 4000. Scorers: Peters, Morgan, Chase, Gunn; Dryden (pen).

Chelsea (0) 2, Watford (1) 2, Stamford Bridge, 4132. Scorers: Weale, Weave; Morris, Brown.

Millwall (0) 1, Tottenham Hotspur (0) 2, The Den, 6000. Scorers: Bell; Broadis 2.

Queen's Park Rangers (0) 1, Crystal Palace (2) 3, Loftus Road, 6900. Scorers: Harris; Smith T 3.

Reading (1) 4, Brentford (2) 3, Elm Park, 5159. Scorers: Cothliff 2, MacPhee, Davie; Townsend, Hopkins, Smith.

West Ham United (1) 2, Charlton Athletic (1) 2, Upton Park, 9789. Scorers: Foxall, Bicknell; Smith, Mason.

27 December 1941

Aldershot (1) 2, Chelsea (2) 3, Recreation Ground, 6000. Scorers: Hagan, Glasby; Weale, Galloway, Kurz.

Brentford (2) 4, Brighton & Hove Albion (1) 2, Griffin Park, 5000. Scorers: Townsend 2, Smith, Tooze (og); Davie, Wilson.

Clapton Orient (3) 3, West Ham United (1) 1, Brisbane Road, 3000. Scorers: Tully 2, Armstrong; Chapman.

Crystal Palace (1) 1, Reading (0) 1, Selhurst Park, 3550. Scorers: Robson; Court.

Fulham (0) 0, Queen's Park Rangers, (3) 3, Craven Cottage, 3771. Scorers: Moore, Mangnall, own goal.

Portsmouth (1) 3, Millwall (1) 2, Fratton Park, 6217. Scorers: Black 2, Guthrie (pen); Mansfield, Osborne.

Tottenham Hotspur (0) 1, Arsenal (0) 2, White Hart Lane, 16,777. Scorers: Ludford; Compton D, Drake.

Watford (0) 1, Charlton Athletic (1) 2, Vicarage Road, 2347. Scorers: Morris; Baxter, Revell.

3 January 1942

Arsenal (1) 6, Portsmouth (0) 1, White Hart Lane, 10,160. Scorers: Lewis 3, Kirchen 2, Flewin (og); Barlow.

Brentford (4) 5, Clapton Orient (0) 2, Griffin Park, 3420. Scorers: Holliday 2, Hopkins, McKenzie, Barnes (og); Armstrong, Poyser (og).

Charlton Athletic (1) 1, Aldershot (1) 5, The Valley, 3011. Scorers: Welsh;
Jones 2, Lawton 2, Hagan.

Chelsea (1) 3, Millwall (1) 3, Stamford Bridge, 3442. Scorers: Peacock, Kurz, Bearryman; Osborne 3.

Crystal Palace (4) 10, Brighton & Hove Albion (0) 1, Selhurst Park, 4771. Scorers: Robson 4, Dawes A 2, Smith 2, Gillespie 2; Stephens.

Queen's Park Rangers (1) 1, Tottenham Hotspur (0) 0, Loftus Road, 4500. Scorer: Mallett.

Reading (2) 4, Fulham (1) 1, Elm Park, 4667. Scorers: MacPhee 2, Edelston, Hall; Gallacher.

West Ham United (2) 4, Watford (1) 1, Upton Park, 4000. Scorers: Wood 3, Foxall; Jones E.

10 January 1942

Aldershot (1) 1, West Ham United (3) 5, Recreation Ground, 3500. Scorers: Pescod;
Chapman 3, Foreman, Quickenden.

Brighton & Hove Albion (1) 3, Fulham (1) 7, Goldstone Ground, 2500. Scorers: Day 2, Cunliffe; Finch 2, Gallacher 2, Rooke 2, Dean.

Chelsea (0) 1, Arsenal (3) 5, Stamford Bridge, 12,260. Scorers: Weale;
Compton L 2, Kirchen 2, Miller.

Clapton Orient (1) 2, Watford (0) 0, Brisbane Road, 1200. Scorers: Dryden, Crawford.

Crystal Palace (1) 2, Brentford (0) 0, Selhurst Park, 6000. Scorers: Barke, Dawes A (pen).

Millwall (0) 0, Charlton Athletic (1) 1, The Den, 6742. Scorer: Welsh.

Portsmouth (2) 3, Queen's Park Rangers (0) 1, Fratton Park, 4251. Scorers: Black, Griffiths, Ward; Mangnall.

Tottenham Hotspur (0) 2, Reading (1) 1, White Hart Lane, 4418. Scorers: Broadis, Burgess; Chitty.

17 January 1942

Arsenal (2) 3, Charlton Athletic (2) 2, White Hart Lane, 3958. Scorers: Kirchen 3; Geldard, Brown.

Brentford (1) 2, Fulham (2) 3, Griffin Park, 3000. Scorers: Smith, Hopkins; Dean 3.

Brighton & Hove Albion (1) 5, Tottenham Hotspur (0) 2, Goldstone Ground, 2000.
Scorers: Morgan 3, Davie, Cunliffe; Burgess, Sibley.

Chelsea (2) 3, Queen's Park Rangers (0) 1, Stamford Bridge, 1829. Scorers: Weale 2, Galloway;
Mangnall.

Clapton Orient (3) 4, Crystal Palace (0) 0, Brisbane Road, 2000. Scorers: Dryden, Tully, Odell,
Fletcher.

Millwall (0) 1, West Ham United (1) 3, The Den, 4000. Scorers: Bell; Chapman, Foxall, Small.

Reading (4) 5, Portsmouth (0) 2, Elm Park, 3888. Scorers: Bradley 4, Cothliff; Barlow, Moores.

Watford v Aldershot postponed.

24 January 1942

Charlton Athletic (3) 3, Queen's Park Rangers (1) 1, The Valley, 2305.
Scorers: Revell 2, Green; Mangnall.

Clapton Orient (0) 0 Aldershot (2) 5, Brisbane Road, 1500. Scorers: Halton 2, Hagan, Jones,
Britton.

Portsmouth (1) 5, Brighton & Hove Albion (2) 3, Fratton Park, 4190. Scorers: Black 2, Barlow,
Guthrie (pen), Risdon (og); Morgan, Welsh Cunliffe.

West Ham United (1) 3, Arsenal (0) 0, Upton Park, 20,000. Scorers: Foreman 2, Goulden.

*Fulham v Crystal Palace; Reading v Chelsea; Tottenham Hotspur v Brentford and Watford v
Millwall all postponed.*

31 January 1942

Arsenal (5) 11, Watford (0) 0, White Hart Lane, 4701. Scorers: Lewis 5, Bastin 2, Compton D 2,
Kirchen 2.

Brentford (0) 2, Portsmouth (3) 5, Griffin Park, 3820. Scorers: Wilkins, Holliday;
Barlow 2, Black 2, Griffiths.

Brighton & Hove Albion (3) 8, Chelsea (1) 2, Goldstone Ground, 2500.
Scorers: Davie 5, Cunliffe 2, Morgan; Thomas 2.

Crystal Palace (1) 2, Tottenham Hotspur (1) 2, Selhurst Park, 5332.
Scorers: Dawes A (pen), Henley; Ludford, Gibbons.

Fulham (3) 5, Clapton Orient (0) 1, Craven Cottage, 1921. Scorers: Conley 3, Dean, Finch;
Armstrong.

Millwall (0) 3, Aldershot (1) 1, The Den, 2000. Scorers: Bell 2, Smith E; Halton.

Queen's Park Rangers (2) 2, West Ham United (0) 1, Loftus Road, 5000.
Scorers: Armstrong, Farmer; Small.

Reading (1) 1, Charlton Athletic (3) 4, Elm Park, 4000. Scorers: Edelston; Welsh 3, Revell.

7 February 1942

Aldershot (0) 1, Arsenal (0) 0, Recreation Ground, 8700. Scorer: Lawton.

Charlton Athletic (2) 8, Brighton & Hove Albion (0) 2, The Valley, 944. Scorers: Revell 3, Green
2, Hobbis, Brown, Mason; Davie, Wilson.

Chelsea (0) 1, Brentford (1) 1, Stamford Bridge, 3135. Scorers: Gibbons; Wilkins.

Portsmouth (1) 3, Crystal Palace (0) 1, Fratton Park, 4515. Scorers: Court 3; Wilson.

*Clapton Orient v Millwall; Tottenham Hotspur v Fulham; Watford v Queen's Park Rangers And
West Ham United v Reading postponed.*

14 February 1942

Arsenal (5) 10, Millwall (0) 0, White Hart Lane, 7520. Scorers: Lewis 4, Nelson 3, Bastin 2 (2 pens), Henley.

Brighton & Hove Albion (0) 1, West Ham U (1) 3, Goldstone Ground, 3000. Scorers: Cunliffe; Foreman, Small, Goulden.

Charlton Athletic (2) 3, Brentford (1) 2, The Valley, 3959. Scorers: Watson, Baxter, Hobbis; Perry, Duncan.

Clapton Orient (0) 2, Tottenham Hotspur (2) 3, Brisbane Road, 4500. Scorers: Barnes, Crawford; Gibbons 3.

Crystal Palace (0) 3, Chelsea (2) 2, Selhurst Park, 5583. Scorers: Robson, Gregory M, Dawes A; Galloway, Townsend.

Fulham (0) 2, Portsmouth (2) 7, Craven Cottage, 4404. Scorers: Conley 2; Barlow 3, Bullock 2, Griffiths, Parker.

Queen's Park Rangers (0) 0, Aldershot (1) 2, Loftus Road, 3086. Scorer: Raynor 2.

Reading (3) 5, Watford (1) 1, Elm Park, 2628. Scorers: MacPhee 2, Edelston 2, Bradley; Kilhourhy.

21 February 1942

Aldershot (0) 0, Reading (0) 0, Recreation Ground, 3752.

Charlton Athletic (1) 3, Crystal Palace (1) 1, The Valley, 2760. Scorers: Hobbis 2, Revell; Barke.

Chelsea (1) 1, Fulham (2) 5, Stamford Bridge, 3255. Scorers: Townsend; Rooke 2, Gallacher, Finch, Woodward.

Clapton Orient (0) 1, Arsenal (2) 3, Brisbane Road, 6000. Scorers: Odell; Lewis 2, Kirchen.

Millwall (0) 1, Queen's Park Rangers (2) 2, The Den, 1000. Scorers: Eastham; Hatton 2.

Tottenham Hotspur (0) 1, Portsmouth (0) 1, White Hart Lane, 4813. Scorers: Gibbons; Griffiths.

Watford (2) 7, Brighton & Hove Albion (1) 1, Vicarage Road, 1000. Scorers: Kilhourhy 2, Jones T 2, Kurz, Jones E, Lewis G; Lancelotte.

West Ham United (2) 2, Brentford (0) 1, Upton Park, 4000. Scorers: Small, Goulden; Hunt.

28 February 1942

Brentford (3) 5, Watford (3) 3, Griffin Park, 3110. Scorers: Hunt 2, Hopkins 2, Smith; Hutton 2, Lancelotte.

Brighton & Hove Albion (0) 1, Aldershot (2) 5, Goldstone Ground, 4500. Scorers: Welsh; Hagan 3, Lawton, Palmer.

Crystal Palace (0) 1, West Ham United (1) 1, Selhurst Park, 7790. Scorers: Robson; Small.

Fulham (2) 4, Charlton Athletic (1) 7, Craven Cottage, 3091. Scorers: Dean 2, Rooke, Gallacher; Tadman 4, Hobbis 3.

Millwall (0) 1, Reading (1) 1, The Den, 3700. Scorers: Fisher (pen); MacPhee.

Portsmouth (6) 16, Clapton Orient (1) 1, Fratton Park, 5010. Scorers: Black 8, Barlow 2, Griffiths 2, Parker 2, Bullock, Guthrie; Barnes.

Queen's Park Rangers (0) 0, Arsenal (0) 1, Loftus Road, 8932. Scorer: Drake.

Tottenham Hotspur (1) 2, Chelsea (0) 0, White Hart Lane, 6558. Scorers: Ludford 2.

7 March 1942

Aldershot (3) 6, Brentford (1) 3, Recreation Ground, 3000. Scorers: Martin 3, Hagan 2, Wright; Hopkins, Hunt, McKenzie.

Chelsea (1) 3, Portsmouth (0) 4, Stamford Bridge, 3258. Scorers: Townsend 3; Black 2, Barlow, Compton L (og).

Mllwall (0) 2, Brighton & Hove Albion (0) 0, The Den, 1000. Scorers: Bell, Osborne.

Queen's Park Rangers (0) 2, Clapton Orient (1) 1, Loftus Road, 2000. Scorers: Hatton, Mangnall; Fletcher.

Reading (0) 1, Arsenal (1) 4, Elm Park, 10,000. Scorers: Stephenson; Lewis 2, Nelson, Compton D.

Tottenham Hotspur (1) 2, Charlton Athletic (0) 0, White Hart Lane, 4641. Scorers: Revell, Gibbons.

Watford (0) 2, Crystal Palace (1) 1, Vicarage Road, 500. Scorers: Halford, Lewis G; Barke.

West Ham United (0) 1, Fulham (0) 1, Upton Park, 2500. Scorers: Goulden; Kiernan.

14 March 1942

Arsenal (2) 4, Brighton & Hove Albion (2) 2, White Hart Lane, 6206. Scorers: Drake 4; Risdon (pen), Morgan.

Brentford (2) 4, Millwall (0) 3, Griffin Park, 3960. Scorers: Hopkins, Smith, Hunt, Cardwell (og); Driver, Heathcote, own goal.

Charlton Athletic (1) 2, Portsmouth (3) 5, The Valley, 4901. Scorers: Hobbis, Lancelotte; Barlow 2, Black 2, Moores.

Clapton Orient (0) 0, Chelsea (1) 3, Brisbane Road, 2000. Scorers: Weaver 2, own goal.

Crystal Palace (1) 1, Aldershot (1) 2, Selhurst Park, 5700. Scorers: Barke; Raynor, Wright.

Fulham (1) 1, Watford (1) 3, Craven Cottage, 2462. Scorers: Finch; Wipfler, Hutton, Jones T.

Queen's Park Rangers (3) 4, Reading (0) 0, Loftus Road, 3400. Scorers: Hatton 2, Mangnall 2.

West Ham United (2) 2, Tottenham Hotspur (1) 3, Upton Park, 7986. Scorers: Fenton, Goulden; Broadis 2, Gibbons.

25 April 1942

Tottenham Hotspur (1) 2, Brentford (1) 1, White Hart Lane, 5131. Scorers: Broadis, Howe; Sneddon.

Watford (0) 1, Aldershot (2) 5, Vicarage Road, 2067. Scorers: Keeton (og); Palmer, Britton, Pescod, Smeaton, Raynor.

West Ham United (1) 2, Reading (0) 1, Upton Park, 4321. Scorers: Mahon, Chapman; Cothliff.

2 May 1942

Clapton Orient (0) 3, Millwall (1) 3, Brisbane Road, 1200. Scorers: Odell, Armstrong, Dryden; Heathcote, Dolding, Harrison.

Reading (0) 3, Chelsea (1) 2, Elm Park, 3128. Scorers: Bradley 2, Edelston; Weaver, Weale.

Tottenham Hotspur (4) 7, Fulham (1) 1, White Hart Lane, 3754. Scorers: Stevens 2, Gibbons 2, Ludford 2, Broadis; Conley.

Watford (0) 0 Queen's Park Rangers (0) 5, Vicarage Road, 1721. Scorers: Heath 2, McEwan 2, Lowe.

9 May 1942
Crystal Palace (3) 3, Arsenal (1) 3, Selhurst Park, 10,024.   Scorers: Dawes A 2, Geldard; Lewis 3.
Watford (0) 1, Millwall (0) 0, Vicarage Road, 1686.   Scorer: Jones E (pen).

23 May 1942
Fulham (0) 4, Crystal Palace (3) 3, Craven Cottage, 3000.   Scorers: Conley 4; Smith JF, Collins,
Lewis G.

LONDON CUP 1941-42

Group 1

21 March 1942
Arsenal (3) 4, Clapton Orient (0) 1, White Hart Lane, 6790. Scorers: Drake 2, Nelson, Compton D;
Fletcher.
Brighton & Hove Albion (1) 1, West Ham United (2) 2, Goldstone Ground, 4000. Scorers: Davie;
Foxall, Foreman.

28 March 1942
Clapton Orient (2) 3, Brighton & Hove Albion (1) 2, Brisbane Road, 1500.
Scorers: Crawford, Armstrong, Fletcher; Lane, Davie.
West Ham United (0) 0, Arsenal (3) 4, Upton Park, 19,000.
Scorers: Drake, Kirchen, Bastin, Nelson.

4 April 1942
Clapton Orient (0) 1, Arsenal (2) 2, Brisbane Road, 6000. Scorers: Crawford; Lewis, Henley.
West Ham United (2) 6, Brighton & Hove Albion (1) 2, Upton Park, 4000.   Scorers: Foreman 3,
Mahon 2, Fenton; Cunliffe, Davie (pen).

6 April 1942
Arsenal (0) 1, West Ham United (2) 4, White Hart Lane, 18,405. Scorers: Compton D;
Goulden 2, Small, Fenton.
Brighton & Hove Albion (2) 5, Clapton Orient (1) 2, Goldstone Ground, 5000. Scorers: Davie 3,
Cunliffe, Griffin; Armstrong, Odell.

11 April 1942
Brighton & Hove Albion (0) 0, Arsenal (1) 3, Goldstone Ground, 12,000. Scorers: Compton D 2,
Drake.
West Ham United (3) 5, Clapton Orient (1) 3, Upton Park, 7000.   Scorers: Foreman 2, Wood 2,
Corbett; Armstrong 2, Dryden.

18 April 1942
Arsenal (3) 5, Brighton & Hove Albion (1) 1, White Hart Lane, 8362. Scorers: Lewis 2, Compton
D, Bastin (pen), Ford (og); Davie.
Clapton Orient (0) 0, West Ham United (0) 1, Brisbane Road, 8000. Scorer: Foreman.

Group 2

21 March1942
Brentford (5) 6, Aldershot (0) 2, Griffin Park, 5120. Scorers: Hunt 2, Wilkins 2, Smith L, Perry;
Maskell 2.
Millwall (1) 2, Queen's Park Rangers (1) 2, The Den, 5000.   Scorers: Bell, Fisher; Hatton 2.

28 March 1942
Aldershot (0) 0, Queen's Park Rangers (1) 2, Recreation Ground, 3000. Scorers: Kirkham, Hatton.
Brentford (2) 3, Millwall (0) 3, Griffin Park, 3500.   Scorers: Perry 2, McKenzie (pen);
Sproston, Heathcote, Burrows.

4 April 1942
Aldershot (1) 2, Millwall (2) 4, Recreation Ground, 3000.   Scorers: Holliday 2;
Heathcote 2, Bell, Burley.
Queen's Park Rangers (1) 1, Brentford (0) 2, Loftus Road, 3000. Scorers: Kirkham;
Cheetham, Hunt.

6 April 1942
Millwall (2) 2, Brentford (1) 2, The Den, 7500.   Scorers: Soo, Heathcote; Cheetham 2.
Queen's Park Rangers (0) 1, Aldershot (2) 2, Loftus Road, 4036. Scorers: Lowe;
Jones, Raynor.

11 April 1942
Brentford (0) 1, Queen's Park Rangers (0) 0, Griffin Park, 7310. Scorer: Perry.
Millwall (4) 4, Aldershot (1) 1, The Den, 6193.   Scorers: Driver, Soo, Fisher, Heathcote; Hagan.

18 April 1942
Aldershot (1) 1, Brentford (1) 3, Recreation Ground, 4000. Scorers: Smeaton;
Smith J, Smith L, Hopkins.
Queen's Park Rangers (1) 2, Millwall (0) 0, Loftus Road,4500. Scorer: Hatton 2.

Group 3

21 March 1942
Reading (1) 1, Tottenham Hotspur (2) 2, Elm Park, 6000. Scorers: Edelston; Ward, Howe.
Watford (1) 1, Charlton Athletic (3) 4, Vicarage Road, 2592. Scorers: Kurz;
Welsh 2, Oakes, Revell.

28 March 1942
Charlton Athletic (0) 1, Reading (0) 1, The Valley, 3520. Scorers: Tadman; Beasley.
Tottenham Hotspur (3) 5, Watford (1) 2, White Hart Lane, 4627. Scorers: Gibbons 2, Broadis,
Ludford, Howe; Kilhourhy, Westcott.

4 April 1942
Charlton Athletic (0) 0 Watford (1) 1, The Valley, 3172. Scorer: Dougall.
Tottenham Hotspur (1) 2, Reading (0) 1, White Hart Lane, 7526. Scorers: Duncan, Ludford;
MacPhee.

6 April 1942
Reading (0) 3, Charlton Athletic (2) 5, Elm Park, 6277. Scorers: Henley 3;
Green 3, Smith, Revell.
Watford (0) 0, Tottenham Hotspur (0) 0, Vicarage Road, 4541.

11 April 1942
Tottenham Hotspur (0) 0, Charlton Athletic (0) 3, White Hart Lane, 9505. Scorers: Smith 2, Green.
Watford (0) 6, Reading (0) 0, Vicarage Road, 2187. Scorers: Kurz 4, Brown J, Kilhourhy.

18 April 1942
Charlton Athletic (4) 4, Tottenham Hotspur, The Valley, 7677. Scorers: Revell, Smith, Geldard,
Tadman.
Reading (1) 3, Watford (0) 0, Elm Park, 3004. Scorers: Henley, Bradley, Cothliff.

Group 4

21 March 1942
Chelsea (1) 3, Crystal Palace (2) 3, Stamford Bridge, 4412. Scorers: Spence, Weaver, Joyner;
Barke, Robson, Dawes A.
Portsmouth (2) 9, Fulham (1) 1, Fratton Park, 6215. Scorers: Barlow 3, Griffiths 3, Bullock 2,
Moores; Kiernan.

28 March 1942
Crystal Palace (0) 0, Portsmouth (2) 2, Selhurst Park, 7329. Scorers: Griffiths, Bullock.
Fulham (0) 1, Chelsea (0) 0, Craven Cottage, 5886.   Scorer: Conley.

4 April 1942
Crystal Palace (0) 0, Chelsea (1) 3, Selhurst Park, 5900.   Scorers: Tennant 2, Smith J.
Fulham (1) 2, Portsmouth (0) 1, Craven Cottage, 5187. Scorers: Conley 2; Moores.

6 April 1942
Chelsea (1) 2, Fulham (1) 2, Stamford Bridge, 10,986. Scorers: Spence, Townsend; Conley 2.
Portsmouth (1) 2, Crystal Palace (1) 1, Fratton Park, 11,671. Scorers: Black 2; Dawes A.

11 April 1942
Fulham (1) 4, Crystal Palace (0) 1, Craven Cottage, 6000. Scorers: Woodward 2, Conley,
Gallacher; Hiles (og).
Portsmouth (0) 2, Chelsea (0) 0, Fratton Park, 8326. Scorers: Black 2.

18 April 1942
Chelsea (0) 0, Portsmouth (0) 0, Stamford Bridge, 7721.
Crystal Palace (1) 3, Fulham (3) 4, Selhurst Park, 3378. Scorers: MacPhee 2, Dawes A (pen);
Rooke 3, Foxall.

Semi-finals
25 April 1942
Charlton Athletic (0) 0, Portsmouth (1) 1, Stamford Bridge, 19,036. Scorer: Black.
2 May 1942
Arsenal (0), Brentford (0) 0, Stamford Bridge, 41,253.

Semi-final replay
16 May 1942
Arsenal (0) 1, Brentford (1) 2, White Hart Lane, 37,600. Scorers: Poyser (og); Wilkins, Hunt.

Final
30 May 1942
Brentford (1) 2, Portsmouth (0) 0, Wembley Stadium, 69,792. Scorers: Smith L 2.

Cup-Winners' Play-off
6 June 1942
Brentford (0) 1, Wolverhampton Wanderers (0) 1, Stamford Bridge, 20,174. Scorers: Collett; Mullen.

On the cover:

Arsenal v Charlton Athletic at White Hart Lane, a time when Highbury was in use for the war effort.

© Popperfoto

RESULTS, LINE-UPS AND SCORERS, CLUB BY CLUB

LONDON CUP 1940-41, 1941-42 and LONDON LEAGUE 1941-42

Throughout this section initials before names denote amateurs.
*Players marked thus * are either unknown guests, local juniors or volunteers from the crowd.*

ALDERSHOT

LONDON CUP 1940-41

Chelsea (home) won 1-0 (Brooks)
Briggs; Keeton, Kelly, Britton, Foster, Bamford, Raynor, Brooks, Ray, Chalmers, Proud.

Chelsea (away) lost 1-5 (Bamford)
Briggs; Keeton, Anderson, Holley, Foster, Dixon, Raynor, Chalmers, Egan, Bamford, Proud.

Queen's Park Rangers (away) won 3-2 (Britton, Bamford, Ray)
Bentley; Keeton, Anderson, Britton, Holley, Bamford, Raynor, Hagan, Ray, Chalmers, J Campbell.

Crystal Palace (home) drew 3-3 (Brooks, Hagan, Raynor)
Briggs; Foster, Keeton, Britton, Walters, Bamford, Raynor, Hagan, Brooks, Chalmers, J Campbell.

Queen's Park Rangers (home) lost 4-2 (Hagan 2)
Briggs; Keeton, Kelly, Britton, Walters, Bamford, Raynor, Hagan, Ray, Fagan, Proud.

Fulham (home) won 3-1 (Dawes A 2, Morgan)
Bentley; Sheppard, Kelly, Smith, Foster, Taylor, Raynor, Ray, Morgan, Dawes, Bamford.

Fulham (home) won 4-2 (Bamford 2, Chalmers, Dawes A)
C Putt; Sheppard, Kelly, Britton, Foster, Taylor, Geldard, Chalmers, Ray, Dawes, Bamford.
(*NB both Fulham games at the Recreation Ground by arrangement*)

Brentford (away) lost 4-2 (Gallacher, Bamford)
C Putt; Sheppard, Kelly, Walters, Foster, Taylor, Raynor, Gallacher, Lawton, Dawes, Bamford.

Brentford (home) drew 2-2 (Raynor, Hagan)
C Putt; Sheppard, Kelly, Britton, Hardwick, Alder, Raynor, Hagan, Lawton, Gallacher, Bamford.

Crystal Palace (away) lost 1-0
C Putt; Sheppard, Kelly, Britton, Walters, Alder, Raynor, Hagan, Dawes, Gallacher, Chalmers.

Appearances: Alder (Rossendale) 2, Anderson (Brentford) 2, Bamford (Brentford) 9, Bentley (Burnley) 2, Britton (Everton) 7, Briggs (Halifax) 4, Brooks 2, J Campbell 2, Chalmers 6, Dawes 4, Dixon 1, Egan 1, Fagan (Liverpool) 1, Foster (Guildford) 6, Gallacher (Bournemouth) 3, Geldard (Bolton) 1, Hagan (Sheff U) 5, Hardwick (Middlesbrough) 1, Holley (Leeds) 2, Keeton (Torquay) 5, Kelly 7, Lawton (Everton) 2, Morgan (Accrington) 1, C Putt 4, Proud 3, Ray 5, Raynor 9, Sheppard 5, Smith (Charlton) 1, Taylor (Bolton) 3, Walters 4 (Chester).

Goals: (21) Bamford 5, Hagan 4, Dawes 3, Brooks 2, Raynor 2, Britton 1, Chalmers 1, Gallacher 1, Morgan 1, Ray 1.

LONDON LEAGUE 1941-42

Fulham (away) won 6-2 (Lawton 2, Hagan 2, Taylor G, Glasby)
C Putt; Sheppard, Kelly, Palmer, Walters, Pescod, H Glasby, Hagan, Lawton, Taylor G, Chalmers.

Tottenham Hotspur (home) won 3-2 (Lawton, Palmer, Britton (pen))
C Putt; Marsden, Kelly, Britton, Walters, Pescod, Raynor, Palmer, Lawton, Halton, Bamford.

Portsmouth (away) drew 2-2 (Neill, Halton (pen))
C Putt; Sheppard, Kelly, Pescod, Walters, Alder, H Glasby, Neill, Halton, Raynor, J Campbell.
Match abandoned 77 minutes; broken goal post.

Chelsea (away) lost 4-0
C Putt; Sheppard, Kelly, Pescod, Walters, Alder, H Glasby, Palmer, Halton, Dawes, Cunningham.

Charlton Athletic (home) won 1-0 (Hagan)
C Putt; Sheppard, Kelly, Pescod, Walters, Halton, H Glasby, Hagan, Lawton, Dawes. Chalmers.

West Ham United (away) lost 3-0
Briggs; Sheppard, Kelly, Bargh, Foster, Taylor G, Raynor, Blair, Dawes, Egan, Chalmers.

Watford (home) won 8-1 (Lawton 3, Hagan 2, Britton (pen), Halton, Raynor)
C Putt; Sheppard, Kelly, Britton, Walters, Pescod, Raynor, Hagan, Lawton, Taylor G, Halton.

Clapton Orient (home) drew 1-1 (Halton)
C Putt; Sheppard, Kelly, Britton, Foster, Pescod, Raynor, Hagan, Lawton, Taylor G, Halton.

Millwall (home) won 5-2 (Halton 3, Raynor, Mahon)
C Putt; Sheppard, Jefferson, Britton, Walters, Taylor G, Raynor, Blair, Brooks, Halton, Mahon.

Arsenal (away) lost 3-2 (Blair, Raynor)
C Putt; Sheppard, Jefferson, Britton, Walters, Taylor G, Raynor, Hagan, Lawton, Blair, Halton.

Queen's Park Rangers (home) won 4-1 (Lawton 4)
C Putt; Kelly Lester, Pescod, Walters, Alsford, Raynor, Dawes, Lawton, Blair, Chalmers.

Reading (away) drew 3-3 (Hagan, Lawton, Blair)
C Putt; Jefferson, Lester, Britton, Walters, Taylor G, Raynor, Hagan, Lawton, Blair, Halton.

Brighton & Hove Albion (home) won 5-1 (Blair 2, Ray, Jones, Campbell JC)
C Putt; Sheppard, Lester, Alsford, Walters, Taylor G, Campbell JC, Raynor, Ray, Blair, Jones.

Brentford (away) lost 5-1 (Britton (pen))
Briggs; Walters, Lester, Britton, Alsford, Gardiner, Raynor, Blair, Brooks, Webb, Jones.

Crystal Palace (home) lost 2-1 (Ray)
C Putt; Sheppard, Lester, Alsford, Walters, Taylor G, Raynor, Egan, Ray, Kinnear, Jones.

Fulham (home) won 4-3 (Geldard 3 1 pen), Lawton)
Briggs; Sheppard, Lester, Dixon, Walters, R Miles, L Monk, Geldard, Lawton, Blair, Jones.

Tottenham Hotspur (away) drew 1-1 (Raynor)
Briggs; Goldberg, Lester, Britton, Walters, Stewart, Raynor, Halton, Lawton, Palmer, Geldard,

Portsmouth (home) won 3-2 (Raynor, Hunt, Glasby)
Briggs; Marsden, Taylor F, Stewart, Halton, Taylor G, Raynor, Hagan, Hunt, Palmer, H Glasby.

Chelsea (home) lost 3-2 (Hagan, Glasby)
C Putt; Marsden, Lester, Stewart, Sheppard, Taylor G, Raynor, Hagan, Chalmers, Palmer, H Glasby.

Charlton Athletic (away) won 5-1 (Lawton 2, Jones 2, Hagan)
C Putt; Kelly, Lester, Britton, Walters, Taylor G, Raynor, Hagan, Lawton, Dixon, Jones.

West Ham United (home) lost 5-1 (Pescod)
Briggs; Kelly, Lester, Britton, Alsford, Sheppard, Raynor, Pescod, Blackman, Halton, Jones.

Clapton Orient (away) won 5-0 (Halton 2, Hagan, Jones, Britton (pen))
Briggs; Sheppard, Lester, Britton, Johnson, Stewart, Ray, Hagan, Lawton, Halton, Jones.

Millwall (away) lost 3-1 (Halton)
Boulton; Sheppard, Lester, Britton, Johnson, Stewart, Raynor, Browne, Halton, Taylor G, Gray.

Arsenal (home) won 1-0 (Lawton)
Briggs; Keeton, Lester, Britton, Johnson, Taylor G, Raynor, Hagan, Lawton, Halton, Jones.

Queen's Park Rangers (away) won 2-01 (Raynor 2)
C Putt; Keeton, Sheppard, Britton, Johnson, Stewart, Raynor, Sibley, Palmer, Smith J, Sabin.

Reading (home) drew 0-0
Briggs; Craig, Sheppard, Britton, Johnson, Taylor G, Raynor, Hagan, Palmer, Stewart. Bonass.

Brighton & Hove Albion (away) won 5-1 (Hagan 3, Lawton, Palmer)
Swift; Sheppard, Lester, Britton, Johnson, Taylor G, Raynor, Hagan, Lawton, Palmer, Bonass.

Brentford (home) won 6-3 (Martin 3, Hagan 2, Wright)
Swift; Craig, Griffiths, Britton, Stewart, Smith J, Raynor, Hagan, Wright, Martin, Bonass.

Crystal Palace (away) won 2-1 (Raynor, Wright)
Briggs; Sheppard, Lester, Stewart, Johnson, Loughran, Raynor, Dixon, Wright, Palmer, Bonass.

Watford (away) won 5-1 (Palmer, Britton (pen), Pescod, Smeaton, Raynor)
C Putt; Keeton, Sheppard, Britton, Stewart, Pescod, Raynor, Smeaton, Palmer, Taylor G, Jones.

LONDON CUP 1941-42

Brentford (away) lost 6-2 (Maskell 2)
Briggs; Craig, Sheppard, Britton, Johnson, Smith G, Raynor, Richardson, Lawton, Maskell, Jones.

Queen's Park Rangers (home) lost 2-0
Grant; Craig, Sheppard, Britton, Smith G, Taylor G, Raynor, Hagan, Lawton, Maskell, Bonass.

Millwall (home) lost 4-2 (Holliday 2)
Grant; Sheppard, Simpson, Loughran, Johnson, Taylor G, Raynor, Dixon, Holliday, Preskett, Jones.

Queen's Park Rangers (away) win 2-1 (Jones, Raynor)
C Putt; Craig, Simpson, Britton, Johnson, Taylor G, L Monk, Raynor, Holliday, Pescod, Jones.

Millwall (away) lost 4-1 (Hagan)
Briggs; Sheppard, Anderson, Britton, Johnson, Stewart, Raynor, Hagan, Brooks, Palmer, Jones.

Brentford (home) lost 3-1 (Smeaton)
Davison; Stewart, Anderson, Britton, Johnson, McCall, Raynor, Wiggins, Court, Smeaton, Jones.

Appearances: Alder (Rossendale) 2, Alsford (ex-Nottm F) 5, Anderson (Brentford) 2, Bamford (Brentford) 1, Bargh (Chesterfield) 1, Blackman (C Palace) 1, Blair (Blackpool) 8, Bonass (QPR) 5, Boulton (Derby) 1, Briggs (Halifax) 12, Britton (Everton) 23, Brooks 3, Browne (Leeds) 1, J Campbell 1, Campbell J (Celtic) 1, Chalmers 5, Court (Cardiff) 1, Craig (Newcastle) 5, Cunningham (Bristol C) 1, Davison (Blackburn) 1, Dawes 4. Dixon 4, Egan 2, Foster (Guildford) 2, Gardiner (RAOC) 1, Geldard (Bolton) 2, H Glasby 6, Goldberg (Leeds) 1, Grant 2, Gray (Lincoln) 1, Griffiths (Chelsea) 1, Hagan (Sheff U) 16, Halton (Bury) 15, Holliday (Brentford) 2, Hunt (Sheff W) 1, Jefferson (QPR) 3, Johnson (Burnley) 12, Jones (Sheff U) 14, Keeton (Torquay) 3, Kelly 11, Kinnear (Rangers) 1, Lawton (Everton) 16, Lester (Sheff W) 15, Loughran (Burnley) 2, Mahon (Huddersfield) 1, Marsden (Bournemouth) 3, Martin (Villa) 1, Maskell (Norwich) 2, McCall (Nottm F) 1, R Miles 1, L Monk 2, Neill (RASC) 1, Palmer 12, Pescod (Easington CW) 11, Preskett (Torquay) 1, C Putt 18, Ray 3, Raynor 31, Richardson (Millwall) 1, Sabin (Cardiff) 1, Sheppard 25, Sibley (Southend) 1, Simpson (Huddersfield) 2, Smeaton (Sunderland) 2, Smith G (Charlton) 2, Smith J (Chelsea) 2, Stewart (Dundee) 12, Swift (Man C) 2, Taylor F (Wolves) 1, Taylor G (Bolton) 20, Walters (Chester) 16, Webb (Brentford) 1,Wiggins (York) 1, Wright (Wolves) 2.

Goals: (93) Lawton 16, Hagan 15, Raynor 10, Halton 9, Britton 5, Jones 5, Blair 4, Geldard 3, Glasby 3, Martin 3, Palmer 3, Holliday 2, Maskell 2, Pescod 2, Ray 2, Smeaton 2, Wright 2, Campbell JC 1, Hunt 1, Mahon 1, Neill 1, Taylor G 1.

ARSENAL

LONDON CUP 1940-41
(NB all home games played at White Hart Lane unless otherwise stated)

Reading (away) lost 2-0
Marks; Male, Scott, Henley, B Joy, Collett, Drake, Jones L, Compton L, Bastin, Compton D.

Reading (home) lost 1-0
Rigg; Male, Scott, Bastin, B Joy, Collett, Kirchen, Drake, Compton L, Curtis, Beasley.

West Ham United (away) won 3-1 (Drake, Curtis, Bastin)
Marks; Male, Scott, Henley, B Joy, Collett, Nelson, Bastin, Drake, Curtis, Compton D.

Clapton Orient (away) drew 3-3 (Compton L, Kirchen, Bastin)
Boulton; Male, Compton L, Henley, B Joy, Collett, Kirchen, Bastin, Drake, Curtis, Compton D.

Clapton Orient (home) won 15-2 (Compton L 10, Bastin 2, Jones L, Compton D 2)
Boulton; Male, Scott, Henley, Collett, Jones L, Nelson, Bastin, Compton L, Beasley, Compton D.

Millwall (away) won 6-1 (Nelson, Crayston, Henley, Compton L 3)
Boulton; Scott, Hapgood, Crayston, B Joy, Collett, Nelson, Henley, Compton L, Bastin, Compton D.

Tottenham Hotspur (away) drew 3-3 (Compton L 2, Kirchen)
Boulton; Drake, Scott, Henley, B Joy, Collett, Kirchen, Lewis, Compton L, Beasley, Nelson.

West Ham United (home) won 3-0 (Drake 2, Compton L (pen))
Boulton; Compton L, Collett, Pryde, B Joy, Henley, Beasley, Curtis, Drake, Bastin, Kirchen.

Tottenham Hotspur (home) lost 3-0
Boulton; Compton L, Hapgood, Pryde, B Joy, Collett, Beasley, Henley, Drake, Bastin, Compton D.

Millwall (away) won 5-2 (Drake 3, Henley, Blakeney)
Boulton; Waller, Beattie, Alsford, Smith L, Collett, Blakeney, Henley, Drake, Bastin, Nelson.
(NB both Millwall games at The Den)

Appearances: Alsford (ex-Nottm F) 1, Beattie A (Preston) 1, Bastin 9, Beasley (Huddersfield) 5, Blakeney 1, Boulton (Derby) 7, Collett 10, Compton D 6, Compton L 8, Crayston 1, Curtis 4, Drake 8, Hapgood 2, Henley 9, Jones L 2, B Joy 8, Kirchen 4, Lewis 1, Male 5, Marks 2, Nelson 5, Pryde 2, Rigg (Middlesbrough) 1, Scott 6, Smith L 1, Waller 1.

Goals: (38) Compton L 17, Drake 6, Bastin 4, Compton D 2, Henley 2, Kirchen 2, Blakeney 1, Crayston 1, Curtis 1, Jones L 1, Nelson 1.

LONDON LEAGUE 1941-42
(NB all home games played at White Hart Lane unless otherwise stated)

Brentford (away) lost 4-1 (Nelson)
Platt; Scott, Hapgood, Jones L, B Joy, Collett, Kirchen, Nelson, Lewis, Bastin, Cumner.

Crystal Palace (home) won 7-2 (Lewis 5, Bastin 2)
Platt; Scott, Hapgood, Crayston, B Joy, Collett, Kirchen, Nelson, Lewis, Curtis, Bastin.

Fulham (away) won 5-2 (Lewis 3, Henley, Kirchen)
Platt; Scott, Hapgood, Crayston, B Joy, Collett, Kirchen, Nelson, Lewis, Henley, Bastin.

Tottenham Hotspur (home) won 4-0 (Cumner 2, Lewis 2)
Platt; Male, Hapgood, Bastin, B Joy, Collett, Kirchen, Nelson, Lewis, Curtis, Cumner.

Portsmouth (away) won 5-1 (Bastin 2, Lewis 2, Henley)
Platt; Scott, Hapgood, Male, B Joy, Collett, Kirchen, Nelson, Lewis, Henley, Bastin.

Chelsea (home) won 3-0 (Lewis, Crayston, Weaver (og))
Platt; Scott, Compton L, Crayston, B Joy, Collett, Drake, Kirchen, Lewis, Nelson, Bastin.

Charlton Athletic (away) won 3-1 (Lewis, Bastin, Crayston)
Platt; Scott, Hapgood, Bastin, B Joy, Collett, Kirchen, Crayston, Compton L, Lewis, Compton D.

West Ham United (homje) won 4-1 (Lewis 2, Kirchen, Compton D)
Platt; Scott, Hapgood, Bastin, B Joy, Collett, Kirchen, Nelson, Lewis, Compton L, Compton D.

Watford (away) lost 3-1 (Beasley)
Platt; Scott, Compton L, Bastin, Smith L, Collett, Kirchen, Beasley, Drake, Curtis, Blakeney.

Aldershot (home) won 3-2 (Miller, Compton D, Lewis)
Marks; Male, Compton L, Crayston, Collett, Jones L, Cumner, Miller, Lewis, Bastin, Compton D.

Millwall (away) drew 2-2 (Miller, Male)
Platt; Goldberg, Compton L, Male, Waller, Collett, Nelson, Miller, Lewis, Jones L, Bastin.

Clapton Orient (home) won 5-2 (Lewis 3, Compton L 2)
Marks; Scott, Hapgood, Crayston, Male, Collett, Drake, Compton L, Lewis, Bastin, Compton D.

Queen's Park Rangers (home) won 4-1 (Compton D 2, Miller 2)
Platt; Goldberg, Compton L, Bastin, Male, Collett, Cumner, Miller, Lewis, Drake, Compton D.

Reading (home) won 3-1 (Lewis 2, Miller)
Platt; Scott, Young, Crayston, Male, Collett, Kirchen, Miller, Lewis, Compton L, Bastin.

Brighton & Hove Albion (away) won 3-2 (Bastin (pen), Drake, Miller)
Platt; Scott, Hapgood, Crayston, Smith L, Bastin, Nelson, Miller, Drake, Curtis, Cumner.

Brentford (home) lost 3-1 (Crayston)
Platt; Male, Scott, Crayston, B Joy, Collett, Drake, Miller, Lewis, Compton L, Bastin.

Fulham (home) won 2-0 (Lewis, Kirchen)
Platt; Scott, Hapgood, Male, B Joy, Collett, Kirchen, Compton L, Lewis, Bastin, Compton D.

Tottenham Hotspur (away) won 2-1 (Compton D, Drake)
Platt; Compton L, Hapgood, Male, B Joy, Collett, Kirchen, Drake, Lewis, Bastin, Compton D.

Portsmouth (home) won 6-1 (Lewis 3, Kirchen 2, Flewin (og))
Platt; Scott, Hapgood, Henley, B Joy, Collet, Kirchen, Bastin, Lewis, Compton L, Compton D.

Chelsea (away) won 5-1 (Compton L 2, Kirchen 2, Miller)
Marks; Male, Hapgood, Crayston, B Joy, Collett, Kirchen, Miller, Compton L, Henley, Bastin.

Charlton Athletic (home) won 3-2 (Kirchen 3)
Platt; Male, Scott, Crayston, B Joy, Collett, Kirchen, Drake, Compton L, Nelson, Bastin.

West Ham United (away) lost 3-0
Platt; Scott, Hapgood, Crayston, Male, Collett, Kirchen, Drake, Lewis, Compton L, Bastin.

Watford (home) won 11-0 (Lewis 5, Bastin 2, Compton D 2, Kirchen 2)
Platt; Scott, Hapgood, Male, B Joy, Collett, Kirchen, Nelson, Lewis, Bastin, Compton D.

Aldershot (away) lost 1-0
Platt; Scott, Hapgood, Male, B Joy, Collett, Kirchen, Nelson, Compton L, Bastin, Compton D.

Millwall (home) won 10-0 (Lewis 4, Nelson 3, Bastin 2 (2 pens), Henley)
Hooper; Scott, Compton L, Crayston, B Joy, Collett, Kirchen, Henley, Lewis, Nelson, Bastin.

Clapton Orient (away) won 3-1 (Lewis 2, Kiernan)
Hobbins; Scott, Hapgood, Crayston, B Joy, Collett, Kirchen, Henley, Lewis, Bastin, Compton D.

Queen's Park Rangers (away) won 1-0 (Drake)
Marks; Scott, Hapgood, Henley, Male, Collett, Drake, Nelson, Compton L, Bastin, Compton D.

Reading (away) won 4-1 (Lewis 2, Nelson, Compton D)
Platt; Scott, Hapgood, Male, B Joy, Collett, Nelson, Crayston, Lewis, Bastin, Compton D.

Brighton & Hove Albion (home) won 4-2 (Drake 4)
Tweedy; Scott, Compton L, Male, B Joy, Collett, Pryde, Nelson, Drake, Henley, Bastin.

Crystal Palace (away) drew 3-3 (Lewis 3)
Tweedy; Male, Collett, Henley, B Joy, Beasley, Drake, Nelson, Lewis, Bastin, Compton D.

LONDON CUP 1941-42

Clapton Orient (home) won 4-1 (Drake 2, Nelson, Compton D)
Marks; Compton L, Hapgood, Male, B Joy, Collett, Pryde, Nelson, Drake, Bastin, Compton D.

West Ham United (away) won 4-0 (Drake, Kirchen, Bastin, Nelson)
Tweedy; Scott, Hapgood, Male, B Joy, Collett, Kirchen, Nelson, Drake, Bastin, Compton D.

Clapton Orient (away) won 2-1 (Lewis, Henley)
Tweedy; Scott, Compton L, Male, B Joy, Collett, Drake, Nelson, Lewis, Henley, Bastin.

West Ham United (home) lost 4-1 (Compton D)
Tweedy; Scott, Hapgood, Male, B Joy, Collett, Drake, Nelson, Lewis, Bastin, Compton D.

Brighton & Hove Albion (away) won 3-0 (Compton D 2, Drake)
Tweedy; Scott, Hapgood, Male, B Joy, Bastin, Nelson, Jones L, Drake, Curtis, Compton D.

Brighton & Hove Albion (home) won 5-1 (Lewis 2, Bastin (pen), Compton D, Ford (og))
Platt; Scott, Compton L, Male, B Joy, Bastin, Drake, Crayston, Lewis, Nelson, Compton D.

Brentford (semi-final at Stamford Bridge) drew 0-0
Marks; Male, Scott, Crayston, B Joy, Collett, Kirchen, Nelson, Lewis, Bastin, Compton D.

Brentford (semi-final replay at White Hart Lane) lost 2-1 (Poyser og))
Platt; Scott, Hapgood, Male, B Joy, Collett, Drake, Drury, Lewis, Bastin, Compton D.

Appearances: Bastin 38, Beasley (Huddersfield) 2, Blakeney 1, Collett 35, Compton D 21, Compton L 23, Crayston 17, Cumner 5, Curtis 5, Drake 19, Drury 1, Goldberg (Leeds) 2, Hapgood 24, Henley 10, Hobbins (Charlton) 1, Hooper (Spurs) 1, Jones L 4, B Joy 29, Kirchen 22, Lewis 28, Male 27, Marks 6, Miller 7, Nelson 24, Platt 24, Pryde 2, Scott 30, Smith L 2, Tweedy (Grimsby) 6, Waller 1, Young 1.

Goals: (128) Lewis 45, Kirchen 14, Compton D 13, Bastin 12, Drake 11, Miller 7, Nelson 7, Compton L 4, Henley 4, Crayston 3, Cumner 2, Beasley 1, Male 1, own goals 4.

BRENTFORD

LONDON CUP 1940-41

Crystal Palace (home) drew 2-2 (Muttitt, Boulter)
Duke; Brown, Poyser, McKenzie, James, Muttitt, Hopkins, Wilkins, Holliday, Boulter, Smith L.

Crystal Palace (away) drew 2-2 (Muttitt, Smith L)
Duke; Brown, Poyser, McKenzie, James, Holliday, Hopkins, Muttitt, Hunt, Wilkins, Smith L.

Chelsea (away) won 1-0 (Davie)
Jackson; Brown, Poyser, McKenzie, James, Holliday, Hopkins, Davie, Hunt, Wilkins, Smith L.

Fulham (away) lost 4-1 (Smith L)
Duke; Brown, Poyser, McKenzie, James, Holliday, Hopkins, Wilkins, Davie, Muttitt, Smith L.

Fulham (home) won 7-4 (McKenzie, Hunt, Hopkins 3, Perry 2)
Duke; Brown, Poyser, McKenzie, James, Holliday, Hopkins, Wilkins, Perry, Hunt, Smith L.

Chelsea (home) drew 2-2 (Smith L, Townsend)
Duke; Brown, Poyser, McKenzie, James, Holliday, Hopkins, Wilkins, Townsend, Hunt, Smith L.

Aldershot (home) won 4-2 (Perry 2, Hopkins 2)
Poland; Brown, Poyser, McKenzie, James, Holliday, Hopkins, Wilkins, Perry, Hunt, Smith L.

Aldershot (away) drew 2-2 (Wilkins, Perry)
Poland; Brown, Poyser, McKenzie, James, Holliday, Hopkins, Wilkins, Townsend, Perry, Smith L.

Queen's Park Rangers (home) won 4-2 (Hopkins, Perry 2, Smith L)
Poland; Brown, Poyser, McKenzie, James, Holliday, Hopkns, Wilkins, Hunt, Perry, Smith L.

Queen's Park Rangers (away) drew 0-0
Jackson; Brown, Poyser, McKenzie, James, Holliday, S Beasley, Smith T, Hunt, Wilkins, Smith L.

Tottenham Hotspur (semi-final away) won 2-0 (Perry, Townsend)
Poland; Brown, Poyser, McKenzie, James, Holliday, Hopkins, Townsend, Perry, Wilkins, Bamford.

Reading (final away) lost 3-2 (Perry 2)
Poland; Brown, Poyser, McKenzie, James, Holliday, Hopkins, Wilkins, Perry, Townsend, Bamford.

Appearances: Bamford 2, S Beasley 1, Boulter 1, Brown 12, Davie (Brighton) 2, Duke (Luton) 5, Holliday 12, Hopkins 11, Hunt (Sheff W) 7, Jackson (Chelsea) 2, James 12, McKenzie (Middlesbrough) 12, Muttitt 3, Perry (Doncaster) 6, Poland (Liverpool) 5, Poyser 12, Smith L 10, Smith T (C Palace) 1, Townsend 4, Wilkins 12.

Goals: (29) Perry 10, Hopkins 6, Smith L 4, Muttitt 2, Townsend 2, Boulter 1, Davie 1, Hunt 1, McKenzie 1, Wilkins 1.

LONDON LEAGUE 1941-42

Arsenal (home) won 4-1 (Wilkins, Smith L, Perry, Hapgood (og))
Jackson; Brown, Poyser, McKenzie, James, Holliday, Hopkins, Wilkins, Perry, Hunt, Smith L.

Queen's Park Rangers (away) won 4-3 (Perry 2, Hunt, Wilkins)
Jackson; Brown, Poyser, McKenzie, James, Holliday, Hopkins, Wilkins, Perry, Hunt, Jones.

Reading (home) won 3-2 (Perry 2, Wilkins)
Jackson; Brown, Poyser, McKenzie, James, Holliday, Hopkins, Wilkins, Perry, Hunt, Smith L.

Brighton & Hove Albion (away) drew 2-2 (Perry Hunt)
Jackson; Brown, Poyser, McKenzie, James, Holliday, Hopkins, Wilkins, Perry, Hunt, Smith L.

Clapton Orient (away) won 3-1 (Perry, Smith L, Hopkins)
Jackson; Brown, Poyser, McKenzie, James, Holliday, Hopkins, Jones, Perry, Hunt, Smith L.

Crystal Palace (home) lost 2-1 (Perry)
Jackson; Brown, Poyser, Muttitt, James, Holliday, Hopkins, Wilkins, Perry, Hunt, Jones.

Fulham (away) lost 4-3 (Townsend, Smale, Perry)
Jackson; Brown, Poyser, McKenzie, James, Holliday, Hopkins, Wilkins, Perry, Townsend, Smale.

Tottenham Hotspur (home) lost 4-1 (Hunt)
Jackson; Brown, Poyser, McKenzie, James, Holliday, Jones, Townsend, Perry, Hunt, Smale.

Portsmouth (away) lost 2-1 (Hunt)
Bartram; Brown, Poyser, McKenzie, James, Muttitt, Smith W, Hunt, Perry, Holliday, Bonass.

Chelsea (home) won 3-1 (Perry, James, Hunt)
Poland; Brown, Poyser, McKenzie, James, Holliday, Hopkins, Townsend, Perry, Hunt, Smith L.

Charlton Athletic (home) won 2-1 (Smith L, Hunt)
Poland; Brown, Poyser, Muttitt, James, Holliday, Hopkins, McCulloch, Perry, Hunt, Smith L.

West Ham United (home) lost 5-0
Duke; Brown, Poyser, Muttitt, James, Holliday, Hopkins, Wilkins, Perry, Hunt, Smith L.

Watford (away) won 6-1 (Perry 4, Hopkins 2)
Poland; McKenzie, Poyser, Aicken, James, Muttitt, Hopkins, Hunt, Perry, Holliday, Smith L.

Aldershot (home) won 5-1 (Hunt 2, Hopkins, Townsend, Duns)
Poland; Brown, Anderson, McKenzie, James, Aicken, Hopkins, Townsend, Perry, Hunt, Duns.

Millwall (away) lost 4-2 (Muttitt, Townsend)
Davison; Brown, Anderson, McKenzie, James, Aicken, Hopkins, Hunt, Townsend, Muttitt, Poyser.

Arsenal (away) won 3-1 (Smirh L, Perry, Duns)
Poland; Brown, Poyser, McKenzie, James, Aicken, Hopkins, Hunt, Perry, Smith L, Duns.

Queen's Park Rangers (home) won 4-3 (Townsend 3, Hunt)
Poland; Brown, Poyser, McKenzie, James, Aicken, Hopkins, Hunt, Townsend, Smith L, Duns.

Reading (away) lost 4-3 (Townsend, Hopkins, Smith L)
Poland; Brown, Anderson, McKenzie, James, Aicken, Hopkins, Wilkins, Townsend, Muttitt, Smith L.

Brighton & Hove Albion (home) won 4-2 (Townsend 2, Smith L, Tooze (og))
Poland; Brown, Harrison, McKenzie, James, Aicken, Hopkins, Wilkins, Townsend, Holliday, Smith L.

Clapton Orient (home) won 5-2 (Holliday 2, Hopkins, McKenzie, Barnes (og))
Rickett; Brown, Poyser, McKenzie, James, Muttitt, Hopkins, Wilkins, Holliday, Smith L, Smale.

Crystal Palace (away) lost 2-0
Poland; Brown, Harrison, McKenzie, James, Muttitt, Hopkins, Hunt, Townsend, Smith L, Duns.

Fulham (home) lost 3-2 (Smith L, Hopkins)
Poland; Brown, Anderson, McKenzie, James, Sneddon, Hopkins, Wilkins, Townsend, Smith L, Duns.

Portsmouth (home) lost 5-2 (Wilkins, Holliday)
Rickett; Brown, Anderson, McKenzie, James, Sneddon, Hopkins, Wilkins, Townsend, Holliday, Smith L.

Chelsea (away) drew 1-1 (Wilkins)
Purdie; Brown, Poyser, Sneddon, James, Muttitt, Hopkins, Wilkins, Perry, Hunt, Smith L.

Charlton Athletic (away) lost 3-2 (Perry, Duncan)
Poland; Brown, Poyser, McKenzie, James, Sneddon, Hopkins, Wilkins, Perry, Hunt, Duncan.

West Ham United (away) lost 2-1 (Hunt)
Poland; Brown, Poyser, McKenzie, James, Sneddon, Hopkins, Wilkins, Perry, Hunt, Muttitt.

Watford (home) won 5-3 (Hopkins 2, Hunt 2, Smith L)
Purdie; Brown, Poyser, McKenzie, James, Holliday, Hopkins, Wilkins, Perry, Hunt, Smith L.

Aldershot (away) lost 6-3 (Hopkins, Hunt, McKenzie)
Poland; Brown, Poyser, McKenzie, James, Sneddon, Hopkins, Hunt, Holliday, Peacock, Muttitt.

Millwall (home) won 4-3 (Hopkins, Smith L, Hunt, Cardwell (og))
Brown H; Brown, Poyser, McKenzie, James, Sneddon, Hopkins, Wilkins, Townsend, Hunt, Smith L.

Tottenham Hotspur (away) lost 2-1 (Sneddon)
Poland; Brown, Poyser, McKenzie, James, Sneddon, Hopkins, Kiernan, Townsend, Hunt, Smith L.

LONDON CUP 1941-42

Aldershot (home) won 6-2 (Hunt 2, Wilkins 2, Smith L, Perry)
Brown H: Brown, Poyser, McKenzie, James, Sneddon, Hopkins, Wilkins, Perry, Hunt, Smith L.

Millwall (home) drew 3-3 (Perry 2, McKenzie (pen))
Poland; Brown, Poyser, McKenzie, James, Manley, Hopkins, Wilkins, Perry, Hunt, Smith L.

Queen's Park Rangers (away) won 2-1 (Cheetham, Hunt)
Polland; Brown, Poyser, McKenzie, James, Sneddon, Hopkins, Wilkins, Cheetham, Hunt, Smith L.

Millwall (away) drew 2-2 (Cheetham 2)
Poland; Brown, Muttitt, McKenzie, James, Sneddon, Hopkins, Wilkins, Cheetham, Hunt, Smith L.

Queen's Park Rangers (home) won 1-0 (Perry)
Poland; Brown, Poyser, McKenzie, W Whittaker, Sneddon, Hopkins, Hunt, Perry, Smith L, Duns.

Aldershot (away) won 3-1 (Smith J, Smith L, Hopkins)
Poland; Brown, Poyser, McKenzie, W Whittaker, Sneddon, Hopkins, Smith J, Perry, Smith L, Duns.

Arsenal (semi-final at Stamford Bridge) drew 0-0
Jackson; Brown, Poyser, McKenzie, James, Sneddon, Hopkins, Wilkins, Perry, Hunt, Smith L.

Arsenal (semi-final replay at White Hart Lane) won 2-1 (Wilkins, Hunt)
Jackson; Brown, Poyser, McKenzie, James, Sneddon, Hopkins, Wilkins, Perry, Hunt, Smith L.

Portsmouth (final at Wembley) won 2-0 (Smith L 2)
Jackson; Brown, Poyser, McKenzie, James, Sneddon, Hopkins, Wilkins, Perry, Hunt, Smith L.

Wolverhampton Wanderers (Cup-winners' play-off at Stamford Bridge) drew 1-1 (Collett)
Jackson; Brown, Poyser, McKenzie, James, Collett, Hopkins, Wilkins, Perry, Hunt, Smith L.

Appearances: Aicken 7, Anderson 5, Bartram (Charlton) 1, Bonass (QPR) 1, Brown H (QPR) 2, Brown W 39, Cheetham 2, Collett (Arsenal) 1, Davison (Blackburn) 1, Duke (Norwich) 1, Duncan (Spurs) 1, Duns (Sunderland) 7, Harrison* 2, Holliday 18, Hopkins 38, Hunt (Sheff W) 33, Jackson (Chelsea) 12, James 38, Jones (WBA) 4, Kiernan (Albion R) 1, Manley 1, McCulloch (Derby) 1, McKenzie (Middlesbrough) 36, Muttitt 13, Peacock (Nottm F) 1, Perry (Doncaster) 27, Poland (Liverpool) 19, Poyser 33, Purdie (Airdrie) 2, Rickett (Chelmsford) 2, Smale (Chelsea) 3, Smith J F (Chelsea) 1, Smith L 30, Smith W (Port Vale) 1, Sneddon (Swansea) 16, Townsend 13, W Whittaker 2, Wilkins 25.

Goals: (102) Perry 20, Hunt 18, Smith L 13, Hopkins 12, Townsend 9, Wilkins 8, Cheetham 3, Holliday 3, McKenzie 3, Duns 2, Collett 1, Duncan 1, James 1, Muttitt 1, Smale 1, Smith J 1, Sneddon 1, own goals 4.

BRIGHTON & HOVE ALBION

LONDON LEAGUE 1941-42

Queen's Park Rangers (home) lost 5-2 (Shafto, Balmer)
Mee; Risdon, Martin, Taylor P, Wilson F, McInnes, Eastham H, Wilson J, Shafto, Balmer, Stephens.

Reading (away) won 5-4 (Balmer 2, Pearson, Taylor P, Tunnicliffe)
Mee; Risdon, Ramsden, Taylor P, Westby, McInnes, Eastham H, Wilson J, Balmer, Pearson, Tunnicliffe.

Clapton Orient (away) drew 3-3 (Easdale, Davie 2)
Mee; Risdon, Westby, Browning, Easdale, Patterson, Eastham H, Wilson J, Davie, Pearson, Stephens.

Brentford (home) drew 2-2 (Wilson J, Balmer)
Mee; Risdon, Ramsden, Taylor P, Westby, Easdale, Eastham H, Wilson J, Balmer, Pearson, Stephens.

Crystal Palace (home) drew 2-2 (Balmer, Ramsden)
Mee; Risdon, Ramsden, Taylor P, Westby, McInnes, Eastham H, Wilson J, Balmer, Patterson, Tunnicliffe.

Fulham (away) won 3-2 (Stephens 2, Davie)
Mee; Risdon, Ramsden, Longdon, Bush, McInnes, Eastham H, Taylor P, Davie, Balmer, Stephens.

Tottenham Hotspur (away) won 2-1 (Balmer 2)
Mee; Risdon, Ramsden, Taylor P, Bush, McInnes, Eastham H, Wilson J, Davie, Balmer, Stephens.

Portsmouth (home) won 2-1 (Jones, Tunnicliffe)
Mee; Risdon, Tooze, Waller, Westby, Browning, Hart, Wilson J, Davie, Jones, Tunnicliffe.

Chelsea (away) won 3-1 (Davie 3)
Mee; Risdon, Clatworthy, Longdon, Westby, Browning, Hart, Wilson J, Davie, Stephens, Tunnicliffe.

Charlton Athletic (home) lost 3-5 (Davie 2, Hart)
Mee; Risdon, Martin, Chase, Longdon, Browning, Hart, Wilson J, Davie, Cunliffe, Stephens.

West Ham United (away) lost 4-0
Mee; Risdon, Lewis, Westby, Wilson F, Browning, Hart, Longdon, Davie, Stephens, Tunnicliffe.

Watford (home) drew 2-2 (Davie, Cunliffe)
Mee; Risdon, Tooze, Waller, Wilson F, Browning, Hart, Curtis, Davie, Morgan, Cunliffe.

Aldershot (away) lost 5-1 (Hart)
Mee; Risdon, Tooze, Waller, Wilson F, Williams, Hart, Wilson J, Westby, Morgan, Cunliffe.

Millwall (home) won 5-0 (Davie 2, Cunliffe 2, Wilson J)
Mee; Marriott, Bowles, Westby, Risdon, Williams, Hart, Wilson J, Davie, Morgan, Cunliffe.

Arsenal (home) lost 3-2 (Davie, Wilson J)
Mee; Risdon, Marriott, Darling, Westby, Longdon, Hart, Wilson J, Davie, Henley, Morgan.

Queen's Park Rangers (away) lost 3-0
Ball; Risdon, Tooze, Jones, Longdon, Williams, Burgess, Wilson J, Chapman, Davie, Mee.

Reading (home) lost 5-1 (Wilson J)
Mee; Risdon, Tooze, Wilson J, Westby, Longdon, Burgess, Cunliffe, Davie, Morgan, Stephens.

Clapton Orient (home) won 4-1 (Peters, Morgan, Chase, Gunn)
Mee; Risdon, Tooze, Chase,.Waller, Malpass, Burgess, Wilson J, Gunn, Morgan, Peters.

Brentford (away) lost 4-2 (Davie, Wilson J)
Mee; A Taylor, Tooze, Risdon, Longdon, Jones, Burgess, Wilson J, Davie, Curtis, Morgan.

Crystal Palace (away) lost 10-1 (Stephens)
Mee; Risdon, Pryde, A Taylor, Longdon, Waller, Chase, Wilson J, Stephens, Thew, Cunliffe.

Fulham (home) lost 7-3 (Day 2, Cunliffe)
Mee; Risdon, Nixon, Chase, Longdon, Dugnolle, Gunn, Davie, Day, Morgan, Cunliffe.

Tottenham Hotspur (home) won 5-2 (Morgan 3, Davie, Cunliffe)
Mee; Risdon, Tooze, Jones, Longdon, Malpass, Williams, Wilson J, Davie, Morgan, Cunliffe.

Portsmouth (away) lost 5-3 (Morgan, Welsh, Cunliffe)
Mee. Risdon, Tooze, Jones, Westby, Malpass, Moores, Eastham G, Welsh, Morgan, Cunliffe

Chelsea (home) won 8-2 (Davie 5, Cunliffe 2, Morgan)
Mee; Risdon, Tooze, Jones, Scrimshaw, Malpass, Williams, Wilson J, Davie, Morgan, Cunliffe.

Charlton Athletic (away) lost 8-2 (Davie, Wilson J)
Mee; Risdon, Tooze, Jones, Scrimshaw, Malpass, Williams, Wilson J, Davie, Morgan, Cunliffe.

West Ham United (home) lost 3-1 (Cunliffe)
Mee; Risdon, Martin, Jones, Longdon, Malpass, Williams, Walker, Davie, Mulraney, Cunliffe.

Watford (away) lost 7-1 (Lancelotte)
Mee; Risdon, Martin, Haworth, Gregory, Ford, Hart, Wilson J, Burdett, Lancelotte, Simmons.

Aldershot (home) lost 5-1 (Welsh)
Mee; Kelly, Martin, Haworth, Risdon, Malpass, Hart, Wilson J, Welsh, Cunliffe, Woods

Millwall (away) lost 2-0
Mee; Kelly, Tooze, Browning, Risdon, Malpass, Buckell, Curtis, Davie, Morgan, Cunliffe.

Arsenal (away) lost 4-2 (Risdon, Morgan)
Mee; Risdon, Tooze, Owens, Ford, Browning, Hart, Wilson J, Davie, Eastham G, Morgan.

LONDON CUP 1941-42

West Ham United (home) lost 2-1 (Davie)
Mee; Risdon, Tooze, Jones, Ford, Browning, Hart, Wilson J, Davie, Eastham G, Morgan.

Clapton Orient (away) lost 3-2 (Lane, Davie)
Kyle; Risdon, Darling, Haworth, Ford, Wilson J, Hart, Lane, Davie, Cunliffe, Ball.

West Ham United (away) lost 6-2 (Cunliffe, Davie (pen))
Mee; Marriott, Tooze, Darling, Ford, Malpass, Hart, Wilson J, Davie, Morgan, Cunliffe.

Clapton Orient (home) won 5-2 (Davie 3, Cunliffe, Griffin)
Ball; Marriott, Bowles, Wilson J, Ford, Malpass, Griffin, Goffey, Davie, Morgan, Cunliffe.

Arsenal (home) lost 3-0
Mee; Thorne, Tooze, Risdon, Ford, Malpass, Griffin, Goffey, Davie, Morgan, Cunliffe.

Arsenal (away) lost 5-1 (Davie)
Woodley; Risdon, Tooze, Jones, Ford, Malpass, Darling, Wilson J, Davie, Morgan, Cunliffe.

Appearances: Ball 3, Balmer (Liverpool) 6, R Bowles 2, G Browning 9, Buckell*1, Burdett* 1, Burgess (Spurs) 4, Bush (Liverpool) 2, Chapman* 1, C Chase 4, Clatworthy (Chelsea) 1, Cunliffe (Hull) 19, Curtis (Arsenal) 3, Darling 4, Davie 26, Day 1, Dugnolle (Plymouth) 1, Easdale (Liverpool) 2, Eastham G (Blackpool) 3, Eastham H (Liverpool) 7, Ford (Charlton) 8, Goffey 2, Gregory F (C Palace) 1, A Griffin 2, A Gunn 2, Hart (T Lanark) 14, Haworth* 3, Henley (Arsenal) 1, Jones S (Arsenal) 10, Kelly (Aldershot) 2, Kyle* 1, Lancelotte (Charlton) 1, Lane (ex-Orient) 1, Lewis (West Ham) 1, Longdon 12, Malpass (Fulham) 12, Marriott 4, Martin 5, McInnes (Liverpool) 5, Mee 33, P Moores (Portsmouth) 1, Morgan (Arsenal) 19, Mulraney (Ipswich) 1, Nixon* 1, Owens * 1, Patterson (Liverpool) 2, Pearson 3, C Peters 1, Pryde (Arsenal) 1, Ramsden (Liverpool) 5, Risdon 34, Scrimshaw (Bradford C) 2, Shafto (Liverpool) 1, L Simmons* 1, Stephens 10, A Taylor* 2, Taylor P (Liverpool) 6, Thew* 1. Thorne 1, Tooze (Arsenal) 17, Tunnicliffe (Bournemouth) 5, Walker C (Sheff W) 1, Waller (Arsenal) 5, Welsh (Charlton) 2, Westby (Blackburn) 12, Williams (Cardiff) 7, Wilson F (Bournemouth) 4, Wilson J 28, Woodley (Chelsea) 1, Woods* 1.

Goals: (82) Davie 27, Cunliffe 11, Balmer 7, Morgan 7, Wilson J 6, Stephens 3, Day 2, Hart 2, Tunnicliffe 2, Welsh 2, Chase 1, Easdale 1, Griffin 1, Gunn 1, Jones 1, Lancelotte 1, Lane 1, Pearson 1, Peters 1, Ramsden 1, Risdon 1, Shafto 1, Taylor P 1.

CHELSEA

LONDON CUP 1940-41

Aldershot (away) lost 1-0
Jackson; O'Hare, Barber, Smith G, Salmond, Griffiths, Spence, Tennant, Kurz, Mills, Foss.

Aldershot (home) won 5-1 (Spence 2, Kurz, Hurley, Galloway)
Jackson; Barber, Smith A J, Macaulay, Salmond, Smith G, Spence, Galloway, Kurz, Tennant, Hurley.

Brentford (home) lost 1-0
Woodley; O'Hare, Smith A J, Macaulay, Salmond, Weaver, Spence, Smith J F, Kurz, Galloway, Tennant.

Queen's Park Rangers (away) lost 5-2 (Tennant, Galloway)
Jackson; O'Hare, Cronk, Macaulay, Smith G, Weaver, Spence, Tennant, Kurz, Galloway, Ferguson.

Crystal Palace (away) drew 3-3 (Galloway, Spence, Kurz)
Jackson; Barber, Cronk, Macaulay, Smith G, Weaver, Spence, Kiernan, Kurz, Galloway, Griffiths.

Brentford (away) drew 2-2 (Kiernan 2)
Jackson; Barber, Griffiths, Tennant, Lyon, Weaver, Spence, Kiernan, Kurz, Mills, Foss.

Crystal Palace (home) lost 3-1 (Kurz)
Jackson; Barber, Griffiths, Tennant, Lyon, Weaver, Spence, Kiernan, Kurz, Smith J F, Milburn.

Fulham (away) lost 4-0
Woodley; Barber, Griffiths, Tennant, Lyon, Weaver, Spence, Kiernan, Mills, Smith J F, Milburn.

Fulham (home) won 4-3 (Malpass (og), Kurz 2, Mills)
Wodley; Barber, Hardwick, Griffiths, Smith G, Weaver, Revell, Smith J F, Kurz, Mills, Spence.

Queen's Park Rangers (home) lost 3-2 (Spence 2)
Jackson; Barber, Hardwick, Griffiths, Smith G, Weaver, Spence, Tennant, Kurz, Mills, Kilduff.

Appearances: Barber 8, F Cronk 2, W Ferguson 1, Foss 2, Galloway (Rangers) 4, Giriffiths 7, Hardwick (Middlesbrough) 2, C Hurley 1, Jackson 7, Kiernan (Albion R) 4, Kilduff (Barrow) 1, Kurz (Grimsby) 9, Lyon (Celtic) 3, J Macaulay 4, G Milburn 2, Mills 5, O'Hare 3, Revell (Charlton) 1, Salmond 3, Smith A J 2, Smith G (Charlton) 6, Smith J F 4, Spence 10, Tennant 8, Weaver 8, Woodley 3.

Goals: (19) Kurz 5, Spence 5, Galloway 3, Kiernan 2, Hurley 1, Mills 1, Tennant 1, own goal 1.

LONDON LEAGUE 1941-42

Charlton Athletic (away) lost 2-1 (Spence)
Woodley; Barber, Hardwick, Macaulay, Vause, Griffiths R, Spence, Smith J F, Kurz, Tennant,
L C Finch.

West Ham United (home) lost 8-4 (Payne, Smith C, Kiernan, Kurz)
Woodley; Barber, Griffiths R, Macaulay, Mayes, Weaver, Smith C, Kiernan, Kurz, Payne, Spence.

Watford (away) won 3-1 (Payne, Kurz, Spence)
Woodley; Hardwick, Johnson, Griffiths R, Vause, Weaver, Smith C, Kiernan, Kurz, Payne, Spence.

Aldershot (home) won 4-0 (Galloway 2, Smith J F 2)
Woodley; Barber, Hardwick, Tennant, Vause, Weaver, Smith JF, Kiernan, Kurz, Galloway, Spence.

Millwall (away) lost 6-3 (Galloway 3)
Woodley; Barber, Hardwick, Tennant, Vause, Weaver, Smith C, Smith J F, Kurz, Galloway,
Spence.

Arsenal (away) lost 3-0
Woodley; Hardwick, Johnson, Tennant, Salmond, Weaver, Smith C, Kiernan, Clements, Galloway,
Spence.

Queen's Park Rangers (away) lost 2-1 (Kurz)
Woodley; Kilpatrick, Smith A J, Tennant, Salmond, Mayes, Smith C, Kiernan, Kurz, Mills, Little.

Reading (away) lost 5-0
Woodley; Muttitt, Griffiths R, Mayes, Salmond, Weaver, Smith C, Kiernan, Tennant, Galloway,
Little.

Brighton Hove Albion (home) lost 3-1 (Galloway)
Jackson; Craig, Hardwick, Tennant, Salmond, Mayes, Spence, Kiernan, Kurz, Galloway, Little.

Brentford (away) lost 3-1 (Tennant)
Jackson; Craig, Hardwick, Griffiths R, Salmond, Weaver, Smith J F, Kiernan, Clements, Tennant,
Little.

Crystal Palace (home) won 1-0 (Wrigglesworth)
Jackson; Craig, Hardwick, Mayes, Salmond, Weaver, Griffiths M, Kiernan, Croom, Tennant,
Wrigglesworth.

Fulham (away) won 4-1 (Smith J F 2, Galloway, Weale)
Jackson; Craig, Hardwick, Tennant, Salmond, Weaver, Griffiths M, Smith J F, Kurz, Galloway,
Weale.

Tottenham Hotspur (home) drew 1-1 (Galloway)
Jackson; Clatworthy, Hardwick, Tennant, Salmond, Weaver, Griffiths M, Foss, McCulloch,
Galloway, Weale.

Portsmouth (away) won 3-2 (Weaver, Weale, Smith J F)
Jackson; Clatworthy, Craig, Tennant, Salmond, Weaver, Spence, Smith J F, Kurz, Galloway, Weale.

Clapton Orient (home) lost 3-1 (Galloway)
Jackson; Clatworthy, Malpass, Tennant, Salmond, Bearryman, Spence, Smith J F, Galloway, Weale, Wrigglesworth.

Charlton Athletic (home) lost 4-2 (Spence, Weale)
Jackson; Craig, Hardwick, Tennant, Salmond, Weaver, Spence, Kiernan, Kurz, Galloway, Weale.

West Ham United (away) lost 5-0
Jackson; Craig, Lewis, Attwell, Salmond, Weaver, Spence, Kiernan, Kurz, Galloway, Weale.

Watford (home) drew 2-2 (Galloway, Weaver)
Jackson; Clatworthy, Hardwick, Tennant, Salmond, Weaver, Spence, Kiernan, Kurz, Galloway, Weale.

Aldershot (away) won 3-2 (Weale, Galloway, Kurz)
Jackson; Craig, Hardwick, Bearryman, Tennant, Weaver, Spence, Dixon, Kurz, Galloway, Weale.

Mllwall (home) drew 3-3 (Peacock, Kurz, Bearryman)
Jackson; Craig, Smith A J, Bearryman, Tennant, Weaver, Spence, Galloway, Kurz, Peacock, Weale.

Arsenal (home) lost 5-1 (Weale)
Jackson; Craig, Hardwick, Tennant, Salmond, Weaver, Spence, Galloway, Kurz, Peacock, Weale.

Queen's Park Rangers (home) won 3-1 (Weale 2, Galloway)
Jackson; Clatworthy, Griffiths R, Tennant, Salmond, Weaver, Spence, Kiernan, Kurz, Galloway, Weale.

Brighton & Hove Albion (away) lost 4-2 (Thomas 2)
Jackson; Craig, Hardwick, Bearryman, Tennant, Weaver, Spence, L C Finch, Thomas, Peacock, Weale

Brentford (home) drew 1-1 (Gibbons)
Jackson; Hardwick, Jefferson, Goslin, Salmond, Bearryman, Spence, Galloway, Gibbons, Peacock, Weale.

Crystal Palace (away) lost 2-3 (Galloway, Townsend)
Jackson; Craig, Griffiths R, Bearryman, Salmond, Weaver, Spence, Tennant, Townsend, Galloway, Weale.

Fulham (home) lost 5-1 (Townsend)
Jackson; Hardwick, Smith A J, Bearryman, Salmond, Aicken, Spence, Tennant, Townsend, Galloway, Weale.

Tottenham Hotspur (away) lost 2-0
Boulton; Clatworthy, Anderson, Bearryman, Salmond, Weaver, Sibley, Galloway, Townsend, Weale, Spence.

Portsmouth (home) lost 4-3 (Townsend 3)
Jackson; Compton L, Hardwick, Tennant, Bearryman, Weaver, Spence, Galloway, Townsend, Bacon, Weale.

Clapton Orient (away) won 3-0 (Weaver 2, own goal)
Jackson; Clatworthy, Hardwick, Tennant, Winterbottom, Bearryman, Joyner, Smith J F, Weaver, Weale, Smale.

Reading (away) lost 3-2 (Weaver, Weale)
Tweedy; Hardwick, Clatworthy, Winterbottom, Dykes, Weaver, Spence, Smith J F, Bearryman, Bacon, Weale.

LONDON CUP 1941-42

Crystal Palace (home) drew 3-3 (Spence, Weaver, Joyner)
Jackson; Clatworthy, Hardwick, Tennant, Winterbottom, Bearryman, Spence, Smith J F, Weaver, Weale, Joyner.

Fulham (away) lost 1-0
Jackson; Hardwick, Anderson, Tennant, Winterbottom, Bearryman, Spence, Smith J F, Weaver, Bacon, Weale.

Crystal Palace (away) won 3-0 (Tennant 2, Smith J F)
Jackson; Clatworthy, Anderson, Winterbottom, Dykes, Weaver, Spence, Smith J F, Tennant, Bacon, Joyner.

Fulham (home) drew 2-2 (Townsend, Foss)
Woodley; Clatworthy, Hardwick, Tennant, Winterbottom, Weaver, Spence, Smith J F, Townsend, Bacon, Foss.

Portsmouth (away) lost 2-0
Jackson; Clatworthy, Hardwick, Bearryman, Winterbottom, Weaver, Spence, Smith J F, Tennant, Foss, Weale.

Portsmouth (home) drew 0-0
Jackson; Clatworthy, Hardwick, Winterbottom, Dykes, Foss, Spence, Macaulay, Tennant, Bacon, Weale.

Appearances: Aicken (Brentford) 1, Anderson (Brentford) 3, Attwell (West Ham) 1, C Bacon 6, Barber 4, Bearryman 14, Boulton (Derby) 1, L Clatworthy 13, B Clements 2, Compton L (Arsenal) 1, Craig (Newcastle) 12, Croom (Leeds) 1, Dixon (Aldershot) 1, Dykes (Hearts) 3, L C Finch 2, Foss 4, Galloway (Rangers) 21, A H Gibbons (Spurs) 1, Goslin (Bolton) 1, Griffiths M (Leicester) 3, Griffiths R 7, Hardwick (Middlesbrough) 25, Jackson 25, Jefferson (QPR) 1, J Johnson 2, Joyner (Sheff U) 3, Kiernan (Albion R) 13, Kilpatrick 1, Kurz (Grimsby) 16, Lewis (West Ham) 1, Little (Doncaster) 4, J Macaulay 3, Malpass (Fulham) 1, Mayes 5, McCulloch (Derby) 1, Mills 1, Muttitt (Brentford) 1, Payne 2, Peacock (Nottm F) 4, Salmond 19, Sibley (Southend) 1, Smale 1, Smith A J 3, Smith C (Aberdeen) 6, Smith J F 14, Spence 29, Tennant 30, Thomas (Plymouth) 1, Townsend (Brentford) 5, Tweedy (Grimsby) 1, Vause (Rochdale) 4, Weale (Burnley) 23, Weaver 29. Winterbottom (Mossley) 8, Woodley 9. Wrigglesworth (Man U) 2.

Goals: (64) Galloway 13, Weale 8, Smith J F 6, Townsend 6, Weaver 6, Kurz 5, Spence 4, Tennant 3, Payne 2, Thomas 2, Bearryman 1, Foss 1, Gibbons 1, Joyner 1, Kiernan 1, Peacock1, Smith C 1, Wrigglesworth 1, own goal 1.

CHARLTON ATHLETIC

LONDON LEAGUE 1941-42

Chelsea (home) won 2-1 (Welsh 2)
Bartram; Cann, Mordey, Smith, John Oakes, Whittaker, Revell, Gibbs, Welsh, Lancelotte, Hobbis.

Clapton Orient (home) won 4-0 (Tadman 2 (1 pen), Revell, Dryden)
Bartram; Cann, Smith, Weightman, John Oakes, Whittaker, Revell, Tadman, Welsh, Dryden, Hobbis.

West Ham United (home) drew 1-1 (Revell)
Bartram; Cann, Green, Weightman, John Oakes, Whittaker, Revell, Smith, Tadman, Lancelotte, Hobbis.

Watford (home) won 5-1 (Hobbis 2, Green, Baxter, Revell)
Bartram; Cann, Jobling, Weightman, John Oakes, Whittaker, Revell, Baxter, Smith, Green, Hobbis.

Aldershot (away) lost 1-0
Hobbins; Cann, Mordey, Weightman, Smith, Jobling, Revell, Green, Welsh, Whittaker, Hobbis.

Millwall (home) lost 2-1 (Revell)
Bartram; Cann Turner, Weightman, John Oakes, Whittaker, Revell, Smith, Tadman, Green, Hobbis.

Arsenal (home) lost 3-1 (Welsh)
Bartram; Cann, Mordey, Weightman, John Oakes, Whittaker, Revell, Baxter, Welsh, Smith, Hobbis.

Queen's Park Rangers (away) drew 0-0
Hobbins; Cann, Shreeve, Weightman, John Oakes, Whittaker, Beasley, Smith, Welsh, Green, Hobbis.

Reading (home) lost 2-3 (Hobbis, Tadman)
Hobbins; Jobling, Shreeve, Weightman, John Oakes, Whittaker, Gee, Smith, Tadman, Hobbis, Revell.

Brighton & Hove Albion (away) won 5-3 (Green 2, Whittaker, Smith, Welsh)
Hobbins; Cann, Jobling, Weightman, John Oakes, Ford, Dryden, Smith, Welsh, Green, Whittaker.

Brentford (away) lost 2-1 (Dryden)
Hobbins; Cann, Jobling, Weightman, John Oakes, Ford, Dryden, Smith, Green, Hobbis, Whittaker.

Crystal Palace (away) lost 4-0
Bartram; Cann, Jobling, Weightman, John Oakes, Ford, Dryden, Smith, Welsh, Green, Lancelotte.

Fulham (home) drew 3-3 (Lancelotte, Ford, Welsh)
Hobbins; Cann, Jobling, Weightman, Smith, Ford, Dryden, Lancelotte, Welsh, Green, Whittaker.

Tottenham Hotspur (home) won 2-1 (Lancelotte, Welsh)
Hobbins; Cann, Phipps, Weightman, Smith, Ford, Revell, Lancelotte, Welsh, Brown, Whittaker.

Portsmouth (away) lost 7-2 (Gibbs, Mason)
Bartram; Cann, Phipps, Weightman, John Oakes, Jobling, Revell, Gibbs, Smith, Mason, Croom.

Chelsea (away) won 4-2 (Welsh 2, Hobbis, Revell)
Bartram; Cann, Phipps, Green, John Oakes, Whittaker, Revell, Smith, Welsh, Mason, Hobbis.

Clapton Orient (away) drew 1-1 (Welsh)
Hobbins; Cann, Phipps, Green, John Oakes, Whittaker, Revell, Smith, Welsh, Mason, Hobbis.
Match abandoned 57 minutes; fog.

West Ham United (away) drew 2-2 (Smith, Mason)
Hobbins; Cann, Phipps, Weightman, John Oakes, Whittaker, Revell, Smith, Green, Mason, Hobbis.

Watford (away) won 2-1 (Baxter, Revell)
Hobbins; Cann, Green, Smith, John Oakes, Whittaker, Revell, Baxter, Welsh, Mason, Hobbis.

Aldershot (home) lost 5-1 (Welsh)
Hobbins; Cann, Hammond, Smith, John Oakes, Whittaker, Green, Baxter, Welsh, Gibbs, Hobbis.

Millwall (away) won 1-0 (Welsh)
Hobbins; Cann, Shreeve, Green, John Oakes, Whittaker, Geldard, Smith, Welsh, Brown, Hobbis.

Arsenal (away) lost 3-2 (Geldard, Brown)
Hobbins; Cann, Shreeve, Baxter, John Oakes, Smith, Geldard, Mason, Tadman, Brown, Hobbis.

Queen's Park Rangers (home) won 3-1 (Revell 2, Green)
Sanders; Turner, Phipps, Green, John Oakes, Whittaker, Geldard, Smith, Revell, Mason, Hobbis.

Reading (away) won 4-1 (Welsh 3, Revell)
Hobbins; Cann, Phipps, Turner, John Oakes, Whittaker, Revell, Smith, Welsh, Mason, Hobbis.

Brighton & Hove Albion (home) won 8-2 (Revell 3, Green 2, Hobbis, Brown, Mason)
Sanders; Cann, Phipps, Turner, John Oakes, Green, Geldard, Mason, Revell, Brown, Hobbis.

Brentford (home) won 3-2 (Watson, Baxter, Hobbis)
Hobbins; Cann, Green, Muttitt, Smith, Whittaker, Revell, Baxter, Welsh, Hobbis, Watson.

Crystal Palace (home) won 3-1 (Hobbis 2, Revell)
Sanders; Cann, Phipps, Green, John Oakes, Whittaker, Geldard, Mason, Welsh, Hobbis, Revell.

Fulham (away) won 7-4 (Tadman 4, Hobbis 3)
Hobbins; Phipps, Lewis, Baxter, John Oakes, Whittaker, Geldard, Mason, Tadman, Hobbis, Revell.

Tottenham Hotspur (away) lost 2-0
Hobbins; Cann, Phipps, Baxter, John Oakes, Whittaker, Geldard, Mason, Welsh, Green, Hobbis.

Portsmouth (home) lost 5-2 (Hobbis, Lancelotte)
Hobbins; Phipps, Whitfield, Turner, John Oakes, Whittaker, Lancelotte, Smith, Green, Etherton, Hobbis.

LONDON CUP 1941-42

Watford (away) won 4-1 (Welsh 2, John Oakes, Revell)
Bartram; Jobling, Shreeve, John Oakes, Dykes, Whittaker, Green, Lancelotte, Welsh, Hobbis, Revell.

Reading (home) drew 1-1 (Tadman)
Bartram; Cann, Shreeve, Green, John Oakes, Whittaker, Geldard, Brown, Tadman, Hobbis, Revell.

Watford (home) lost 1-0
Bartram; Cann, Phipps, Jobling, Smith, Whittaker, Geldard, Green, Revell, Hobbis, Foxall.

Reading (away) won 5-3 (Green 3, Smith, Revell)
Bartram; Cann, Phipps, Turner, John Oakes, Whittaker, Geldard, Smith, Green, Hobbis, Revell.

Tottenham Hotspur (away) won 3-0 (Smith 2, Green)
Hobbins; Cann, Catlin, Phipps, John Oakes, Whittaker, Geldard, Smith, Green, Baxter, Revell.

Tottenham Hotspur (home) won 4-0 (Revell, Smith, Geldard, Tadman)
Bartram; Cann, Catlin, Baxter, John Oakes, Whittaker, Geldard, Smith, Tadman, Hobbis, Revell.

Portsmouth (semi-final at Stamford Bridge) lost 1-0
Bartram; Cann, Catlin, Green, John Oakes, Whittaker, Geldard, Smith, Tadman, Mason, Hobbis.

Appearances: Bartram 15, Baxter (Barnsley) 10, Beasley (Huddersfield) 1, Brown 5, Cann 32, Catlin (Sheff W) 3, Croom (Leeds) 1, Dryden 5, Dykes (Hearts) 1, P Etherton 1, Ford 5, Foxall (West Ham) 1, Gee (Birmingham) 1, Geldard (Bolton) 13, Gibbs 3, Green 27, Hammond 1, Hobbins 19, Hobbis 31, Jobling 10, Lancelotte 7, Lewis (West Ham) 1, Mason (T Lanark) 13, Muttitt (Brentford) 1, Mordey 3, John Oakes 32, H Phipps 15, Revell 26, J Sanders 3, Shreeve 6, Smith 31, Tadman G 9, Turner 6, G Watson (RAF) 1, Weightman (Notts Co) 15, Welsh 19, R Whitfield 1, Whittaker 33.

Goals: (89) Revell 16, Welsh 16, Hobbis 12, Green 10, Tadman 9, Smith 6, Baxter 3, Lancelotte 3, Mason 3, Brown 2, Dryden 2, Geldard 2, Ford 1, Gibbs 1, John Oakes 1, Watson 1, Whittaker 1.

CLAPTON ORIENT

LONDON CUP 1940-41

Tottenham Hotspur (away) lost 3-0
Hall; Wade, Jobling, Johnson, Bartlett, Fletcher C, Tully, Astley, Reeves, Rawlings, Goodman.

Tottenham Hotspur (home) lost 1-9 (Fletcher C)
Wright W P; Jobling, Wade, Smith H, Bartlett, Levene, Silver, Tully, Jobson, Astley, Fletcher C.

Reading (home) lost 4-0
Hillam; Jobling, Wade, Weightman, Bartlett, Black, Tully, Fisher, Astley, Rawlings, Fletcher C.

Arsenal (home) drew 3-3 (McNeil 3)
Hillam; Jobling, Wade, Fletcher C, Bartlett, Black, Tully, Fisher, McNeil, Astley, Rawlings.

Arsenal (away) lost 15-2 (Rawlings, McNeil)
MacIlroy; Jobling, Wade, Fletcher C, Bartlett, Collier, Rawlings, Sargent, McNeil, Fisher, Tully.

Millwall (home) lost 1-0
Hall; Jobling, Wade, Black, Bartlett, Weightman, Tully, Rawlings, McNeil, Fisher, Fletcher C.

Reading (away) lost 9-0
Hall; Wright W, Wade, Ãllum, Bartlett, Weightman, Jenkins, Rawlings, Fletlcher C, Fisher, Tully.

Millwall (away) lost 4-0
Hall; Wright W, Wade, Ross, Bartlett, Gibson, Birdseye, Rawlings, Fisher, Muller, Tully.

West Ham United (away) lost 8-1 (Rawlings)
Hall; Wade, Brooks, Wright W P, Bartlett, Weightman, Tully, Fisher, Crawford, Rawlings, Eaton.

West Ham United (home) lost 3-2 (Fisher, Fletcher C)
Hall; Lunn, Wade, Barnes, Bartlett, Weightman, Tully, Rawlings, Crawford, Fisher, Fletcher C.

Appearances: Allum 1, Astley (Blackpool) 4, Barnes 1, Bartlett 10, F Birdseye 1, Black 3, Brooks (C Palace) 1, H Collier 1, Crawford 2, Eaton* 1, A Fisher (Arsenal) 8, Fletcher C (Ipswich) 8, Gibson* 1, A Goodman 1, Hall 6, Hillam (Southend) 2, Jenkins* 1, Jobling (Charlton) 6, Jobson 1, Johnson* 1, Levene 1, Lunn (A Villa) 1, MacIlroy* 1, McNeil 3, Muller* 1, J Rawlings 9, Reeves (Grimsby) 1, Ross (Leith Ath) 1, C Sargent 1, H Silver 1, Smith H 1, Tully 10, Wade (ex-Aldershot) 10, Weightman (Notts Co) 5, Wright W 2, Wright W P (Manager) 2.

Goals: (9) McNeil 4, Fletcher 2, Rawlings 2, Fisher 1.

LONDON LEAGUE 1941-42

Reading (home) lost 8-3 (Armstrong 2, Fletcher)
Ellis; Barford, McDonald, Allum, Bartlett, Levene, Nicholls, Willshaw, Armstrong, Crawford, Fletcher.

Charlton Athletic)away) lost 4-0
Hall; Lunn, Jobling, Fletcher, Bartlett, Black, Willshaw, Odell, Armstrong, Crawford, Tully.

Brighton & Hove Albion (home) drew 3-3 (Willshaw 2, Crawford)
Hall; Lunn, Rumbold, Barnes, Bartlett, Black, Bestwick, Willshaw, Crawford, Fletcher, Tully.

West Ham United (away) lost 3-1 (Willshaw)
Hall; Thorogood, Brooks, Barnes, Bartlett, Fletcher, Bestwick, Crawford, Armstrong, Fisher, Willshaw.

Brentford (home) lost 3-1 (Fletcher)
Hall; Thorogood, Brooks, Barnes, Bartlett, Wright W P, Bestwick, Crawford, Willshaw, Fletcher Tully.

Watford (away) drew 2-2 (Bestwick, Willshaw)
Hall; Thorogood, Brooks, Barnes, Bartlett, Fletcher, Bestwick, Odell, Armstrong, Willshaw, Crawford.

Crystal Palace (away) lost 2-0
Hall; Parry, Brooks, Barnes, Bartlett, Aicken, Bestwick, Odell, Crawford, Willshaw, Tully.

Aldershot (away) drew 1-1 (Crawford)
Hall; Brooks, Rumbold, Aicken, Bartlett, Barnes, Woodroffe, Odell, Crawford, Fletcher, Tully.

Fulham (home) won 2-1 (Willshaw 2)
Hall; Thorogood, Brooks, Aicken, Bartlett, Barnes, Bestwick, Odell, Crawford, Willshaw, Tully.

Millwall (away) drew 2-2 (Willshaw 2)
Hall; Allum, Brooks, Aicken, Bartlett, Barnes, Crawford, Odell, Willshaw, Fletcher, Tully.

Tottenham Hotspur (away) lost 2-0
Hall; Lunn, Brooks, Aicken, Bartlett, Barnes, Tully, Odell, Willshaw, Fletcher, Crawford.

Arsenal (away) lost 5-2 (Armstrong 2)
Hall; Allum, Brooks, Aicken, Bartlett, Barnes, Crawford, Odell, Armstrong, Willshaw, Fletcher.

Portsmouth (home) lost 4-0
Hall; Anderson, Brooks, Summerbee, Bartlett, Barnes, Jones, Allum, Willshaw, Fletcher, Crawford.

Queen's Park Rangers (home) drew 0-0
Hall; Allum, Brooks, Barnes, Bartlett, Black, Tully, Wilshaw, Ellis, Fletcher, Crawford.

Chelsea (away) won 3-1 (Willshaw, Odell, Armstrong)
Hall; Allum, Brooks, Barnes, Bartlett, Fletcher, Tully, Odell, Armstrong, Woodroffe, Willshaw.

Reading (away) lost 2-0
Hall; Allum, Brooks, Barnes, Bartlett, Black, Tully, Phillips, Armstrong, Fletcher, Crawford.

Charlton Athletic (home) drew 1-1 (Tully)
Hall; Allum, Brooks, Barnes, Bartlett, Black, Tully, Odell, Armstrong, Fletcher, Crawford.
Match abandoned 55 minutes; fog.

Brighton & Hove Albion (away) lost 4-1 (Dryden (pen))
Hall; Black, Thorogood, Fletcher, Reynolds, Barnes, Willshaw, Dryden, Armstrong, Lucas, Crawford.

West Ham United (home) won 3-1 (Tully 2, Armstrong|)
Hall; Allum, Thorogood, Barnes, Bartlett, Black, Griffin, Crawford, Armstrong, Fletcher, Tully.

Brentford (away) lost 5-2 (Armstrong, Poyser (og))
Hall; Allum, Brooks, Barnes, Bartlett, Thorogood, Griffin, Crawford, Armstrong, Fletcher, Tully.

Watford (home) won 2-0 (Dryden, Crawford)
Hall; Allum, Brooks, Barnes, Bartlett, Black, Crawford, Lucas, Dryden, Fletcher, Tully.

Crystal Palace (home) won 4-0 (Dryden, Tully, Odell, Fletcher)
Hall; Allum, Brooks, Barnes, Bartlett, Black, Tully, Odell, Dryden, Fletcher, Crawford.

Aldershot (home) lost 5-0
Hall; Allum, Brooks, Barnes, Bartlett, Black, Tully, Dryden, Armstrong, Crawford, Strauss.

Fulham (away) lost 5-1 (Armstrong)
Hall; Allum, Brooks, Barnes, Bartlett, Odell, Strauss, Dryden, Armstrong, Crawford, Tully.

Tottenham Hotspur (home) lost 3-2 (Barnes, Crawford)
Hall; Allum, Brooks, Austin, Bartlett, Black, Tully, Barnes, Dryden, Odell, Crawford.

Arsenal (home) lost 3-1 (Odell)
Hall; Brooks, Black, Barnes, Bartlett, Fletcher, Willshaw, Dryden, Armstrong, Odell, Crawford.

Portsmouth (away) lost 16-1 (Barnes)
Hedges; Brooks, Black, Barnes, Bartlett, Fletcher, Tully, Dryden, Armstrong, Brown, Crawford.

Queen's Park Rangers (away) lost 2-1 (Fletcher)
Wright W P: Brooks, Black, Aicken, Bartlett, Barnes, Tully, Odell, Dryden, Fletcher, Crawford.

Chelsea (home) lost 3-0
Hall; Brooks, Black, Aicken, Bartlett, Barnes, Griffin, Odell, Armstrong, Crawford, Tully.

Millwall (home) drew 3-3 (Odell, Armstrong, Dryden)
Hall; Brooks, Kelly, Barnes, Bartlett, Black, Dryden, Odell, Armstrong, Curtis, Crawford.

LONDON CUP 1941-42

Arsenal (away) lost 4-1 (Fletcher)
Hall; Brooks, Kelly, Aicken, Bartlett, Barnes, Griffin, Rankin, Dryden, Fletcher, Tully.

Brighton & Hove Albion (home) won 3-2 (Crawford, Armstrong, Fletcher)
Hall; Brooks, Kelly, Aicken, Bartlett, Barnes, Griffin, Odell, Armstrong, Fletcher, Crawford.

Arsenal (home) lost 2-1 (Crawford)
Hall; Brooks, Kelly, Aicken, Bartlett, Fletcher, Griffin, Odell, Armstrong, Dryden, Crawford.

Brighton & Hove Albion (away) lost 5-2 (Armstrong, Odell)
Hall; Thorogood, Brooks, Aicken, Bartlett, Silver, Griffin, Odell, Armstrong, Dryden, Crawford.

West Ham United (away) lost 5-3 (Armstrong 2, Dryden)
Hall; Brooks, Kelly, Aicken, Bartlett, Barnes, Fletcher, Odell, Armstrong, Dryden, Crawford.

West Ham United (home) lost 1-0
Hall; Rumbold, Kelly, Aicken, Bartlett, Black, Tully, Dryden, Armstrong, Fletcher, Crawford.

Appearances: Aicken (Brentford) 14, Allum 15, Anderson (Brentford) 1, Armstrong (Aberdeen) 22, Austin* 1, Barford* 1, Barnes 31, Bartlett 35, Bestwick* 6, Black 17, Brooks (ex-Palace) 30, Brown* 1, Crawford 34, Curtis (Arsenal) 1, Dryden 15, Ellis 2, A Fisher (Arsenal) 1, Fletcher C 28; Griffin* 7, Hall 33, Hedges (RAOC) 1, Jobling (Charlton) 1, Jones (WBA) 1, Kelly (Aldershot) 6, Levene 1, Lucas* 2, Lunn (Villa) 3, McDonald* 1, Nicholls* 1, Odell (Darlington) 21, Parry (Ipswich) 1, Phillips* 1, Rankin* 1, Reynolds* 1, Rumbold 3, H Silver 1, Summerbee (Preston) 1, Strauss (Aberdeen) 2, Thorogood* 8, Tully 24, Willshaw 16, Woodroffe* 2, Wright W P 2.

Goals: (52) Armstrong 13, Willshaw 9, Crawford 6, Fletcher 6, Dryden 5, Odell 5, Tully 4, Barnes 2, Bestwick 1, own goal 1.

CRYSTAL PALACE

LONDON CUP 1940-41

Brentford (away) drew 2-2 (Dawes A 2)
Tootill; Gregory M, Dawes F, Blackman, Millbank, Collins, Gillespie, Smith, Robson, Dawes A, Ridley.

Brentford (home) drew 2-2 (Dawes A, Robson)
Tootill; Gregory M, Dawes F, Blackman, Millbank, Collins, Waite, Smith, Robson, Dawes A, Wilson A.

Fulham (home) won 5-2 (Dawes A 3, Robson, Smith)
Tootill; Hudgell, Dawes F, Collins, Gregory M, Halliday, Blackman, Smith, Robson, Dawes A, Gillespie.

Aldershot (away) drew 3-3 (Smith, Blackman, Robson)
Tootill; Hudgell, Dawes F, Collins, Gregory M, Halliday, Blackman, Smith, Robson, Dawes A, Gillespie.

Chelsea (home) 3-3 (Blackman, Robson, Dawes A)
Tootill; Hudgell, Dawes F, Gregory M, Millbank, Collins, Blackman, Smith, Robson, Dawes A, Wilson A.

Fulham (away) won 4-1 (Robson 4)
Jackson; Hudgell, Dawes F, Gregory M, Millbank, Collins, R Wilson, Smith, Robson, Blackman, Wilson A.

Chelsea (away) won 3-1 (Wilson A 2, Robson)
Tootill; Hudgell, Dawes F, Gregory M, Millbank, Collins, Revill, Smith, Robson, Blackman, Wilson A.

Queen's Park Rangers (home) lost 2-1 (Blackman)
Tootill; Hudgell, Dawes F, Gregory M, Millbank, Collins, Gillespie, Smith, Robson, Blackman, Wilson A.

Aldershot (home) won 1-0 (Robson)
Tootill; Hudgell, Dawes F, Gregory M, Millbank, Collins, Revill, Waite, Robson, Blackman, Gillespie.

Queen's Park Rangers (away) lost 2-1 (Robson)
Tootill; Hudgell, Dawes F, Lievesley, Gregory M, Collins, Gillespie, Smith, Robson, Blackman, Wilson A.

Reading (semi-final away) lost 4-1 (Blackman)
Tootill; Hudgell, Dawes F, Gregory M, Millbank, Collins, Blackman, Smith, Robson, Barke, Wilson A.

Appearances: Barke 1, Blackman 11, Collins 11, Dawes A (Aldershot) 5, Dawes F 11, Gillespie 6, Gregory M 11, W Halliday 2, Hudgell 9, Jackson (Chelsea) 1, Lievesley 1, Millbank 8, J Revill 2, T Ridley 1, Robson 11, Smith J T 10, Tootill 10, E Waite 2, Wilson A 7, R Wilson 1.

Goals: (26) Robson 11, Dawes A 7, Blackman 4, Smith 2, Wilson A 2.

LONDON LEAGUE 1941-42

Millwall (home) won 2-0 (Robson, Gillespie)
Tootill; Hudgell, Dawes F, Gregory M, Millbank, Collins, Gillespie, Smith J T, Robson, Barke, Wilson A.

Arsenal (away) lost 7-2 (Hawke, Robson)
Tootill; Hudgell, Dawes F, Blackman, Gregory M, Collins, Gillespie, Smith J T, Robson, Hawke, Wilson A.

Queen's Park Rangers (home) won 2-1 (Robson, Dawes A)
Tootill; Hudgell, Dawes F, Gregory M, Millbank, Collins, Blackman, Dawes A, Robson, Barke, Wilson A.,

Reading (away) lost 6-2 (Robson, Blackman)
Tootill; Hudgell, Dawes F, Gregory M, Fuller, Collins, Gillespie, Hawke, Robson, Blackman, Wilson A.

Brighton & Hove Albion (away) drew 2-2 (Hudgell (pen), Robson)
Tootill; Hudgell, Dawes F, Gregory M, Millbank, Collins, Raynor, Gillespie, Robson, Barke, Wilson A.

Brentford (away) won 2-1 (Blackman, Smith J T)
Tootill; Hudgell, Dawes F, Gregory M, Millbank, Collins, Gillespie, Smith J T, Blackman, Barke, Wilson A.

Clapton Orient (home) won 2-0 (Wilson, Dawes A)
Tootill; Hudgell, Dawes F, Gregory M, Millbank, Collins, Gillespie, Dawes A, Blackman, Barke, Wilson A.

Fulham (home) won 3-1 (Robson 2, Barke)
Tootill; Hudgell, Dawes F, Gregory M, Millbank, Collins, Gillespie, Smith J T, Robson, Barke, Wilson A.

Tottenham Hotspur (away) drew 1-1 (Robson)
Tootill; Lester, Dawes F, Gregory M, Millbank, Collins, Blackman, Smith J T, Robson, Gillespie, Wilson A.

Portsmouth (home) won 3-1 (Robson 2, Collins)
Tootill; Hudgell, Dawes F, Gregory M, Millbank, Collins, Dawes A, Smith J T, Robson, Barke, Wilson A.

Chelsea (away) lost 1-0
Tootill; Hudgell, Dawes F, Gregory M, Millbank, Collins, Blackman, Smith J T, Robson, Barke, Wilson A.

Charlton Athletic (home) won 4-0 (Robson 2, Gillespie 2)
Tootill; Hudgell, Dawes F, Gregory M, Morris, Collins, Gillespie, Smith J T, Robson, Dawes A, Wilson A.

West Ham United (away) won 5-0 (Barke 2, Blackman, Gillespie, Robson)
Tootill; Dawes A, Hudgell, Gregory M, Morris, Collins, Blackman, Gillespie, Robson, Barke, Wilson A.

Watford (home) won 6-1 (Barke 2, Dawes A, Gillespie, Blackman, Wilson)
Tootill; Gregory F, Hudgell, Dawes A, Morris, Collins, Blackman, Gillespie, Robson, Barke, Wilson A.

Aldershot (away) won 2-1 (Robson, Collins)
Tootill; Young, Hudgell, Reece, Morris, Collins, Blackman, Smith J T, Robson, Gillespie, Wilson A.

Millwall (away) lost 1-0
Tootill; Hudgell, Dawes F, Reece, Morris, Collins, Sibley, Gillespie, Robson, Blackman, Wilson A.

Queens Park Rangers (away) won 3-1 (Smith J T 3)
Tootill; Hudgell, Dawes F, Morris, Millbank, Collins, Blackman, Smith J T, Robson, Dawes A, Gillespie.

Reading (home) drew 1-1 (Robson)
Tootill; Dawes A. Hudgell, Morris, Millbank, Collins, Blackman, Smith J T, Robson, Gillespie, Wilson A.

Brighton & Hove Albion (home) won 10-1 (Robson 4, Dawes A 2, Smith J T 2, Gillespie 2)
Tootill; Dawes A, Hudgell, Chivers, Morris, Collins, Blackman, Smith J T, Robson, Gillespie, Wilson A.

Brentford (home) won 2-0 (Dawes A (pen), Barke)
Tootill; Scaife, Hudgell, Gregory M, Morris, Collins, Dawes A, Smith J T, Robson, Barke, Wilson A.

Clapton Orient (away) lost 4-0
Tootill; Hudgell, Dawes F, Muttitt, Morris, Collins, Wilson A, Dawes A, Robson, Smith J T, Gillespie.

Tottenham Hotspur (home) drew 2-2 (Dawes A (pen), Henley)
Bartram; Hudgell, Dawes F, Gregory M, Morris, Collins, Dawes A, Smith J T, Robson, Henley, Gillespie.

Portsmouth (away) lost 3-1 (Wilson)
Tootill; Hudgell, Dawes F, Henley, Morris, Collins, Gillespie, Smith J T, Robson, Dawes A, Wilson A.

Chelsea (home) won 3-2 (Robson, Gregory M, Dawes A)
Tootill; Hudgell, Dawes F, Gregory M, Morris, Collins, Blackman, Dawes A, Robson, Barke, Wilson A.

Charlton Athletic (away) lost 3-1 (Barke)
Boulton; Hudgell, Dawes F, Gregory M, Morris, Collins, Gillespie, Smith J T, Robson, Barke, Wilson A.

West Ham United (home) drew 1-1 (Robson)
Bartram; Hudgell, Dawes F, Gregory M, Morris, Collins, Dawes A, Smith J T, Robson, Barke, Wilson A.

Watford (away) lost 2-1 (Barke)
Tootill; Hudgell, Dawes F, Henley, Morris, Collins, Blackman, Smith J T, Robson, Barke, Dawes A.

Aldershot (home) lost 2-1 (Barke)
Tootill; Hudgell, Dawes F, Gregory M, Morris, Collins, Gillespie, Smith J T, Robson, Barke, Dawes A.

Arsenal (home) drew 3-3 (Dawes A 2, Geldard)
Hooper; Hudgell, Dawes F, Gregory M, John Oakes, Collins, Geldard, Duncan, Robson, Dawes A, Wilson A.

Fulham (away) lost 4-3 (Smith J F, Collins, Lewis G)
Tootill; Hudgell, Catlin, Lewis J, Hitchins, Collins, Smith J F, Gillespie, Robson, Lewis G, Wilson A.

LONDON CUP 1941-42

Chelsea (away) drew 3-3 (Barke, Robson, Dawes A)
Tweedy; Hudgell, Dawes F, Dawes A, Morris, Collins, Gillespie, Smith J T, Robson, Barke, Wilson A.

Portsmouth (home) lost 2-0
Hobbins; Hudgell, Dawes F, Gregory M, Morris, Collins, Dawes A, Smith J T, Robson, Barke, Wilson A.

Chelsea (home) lost 3-0
Hobbins; Hudgell, Dawes F, Mathers, Morris, Collins, Gillespie, Mulligan, Robson, Dawes A, Weale.

Portsmouth (away) lost 2-1 (Dawes A)
Tootill; Hudgell, Dawes F, Gregory M, Morris, Collins, Blackman, Robson, Forder, Dawes A, Gillespie.

Fulham (away) lost 4-1 (Hiles og))
Tootill; Hudgell, Dawes F, Gregory M, Morris, Collins, Blackman, Muttitt, Forder, Dawes A, Gillespie.

Fulham (home) lost 4-3 (MacPhee 2, Dawes A (pen))
Tootill; Hudgell, Dawes F, Gregory M, Morris, Collins, Wilson A, Dawes A, MacPhee, Barke, Halford.

Appearances: Barke 19, Bartram (Charton) 2, Blackman 18, Boulton (Derby) 1, Catlin (Sheff W) 1, G Chivers 1, Collins 36, Dawes A (Aldershot) 24, Dawes F 29, Duncan (Spurs) 1, Forder 2, C Fuller (Walthamstow) 1, Geldard (Bolton) 1, Gillespie 26, Gregory F 1, Gregory M 24, Halford (Oldham) 1, Hawke (WBA) 2, Henley (Arsenal) 3, Hitchins (Spurs) 1, Hobbins (Charlton) 2, Hooper (Spurs) 1, Hudgell 35, Lester (Sheff W) 1, Lewis G 1, Lewis J 1, MacPhee (Reading) 1, Mathers (St Johnstone) 1, Millbank 11, Morris 23, Mulligan (Villa) 1, Muttitt (Brentford) 2, John Oakes 1, Raynor (Aldershot) 1, Reece 2, Robson 32, Scaife (Leeds) 1, Sibley (Southend) 1, Smith J F (Chelsea) 1, Smith J T 22, Tweedy (Grimsby) 1, Tootill 29, Weale (Burnley) 1, Wilson A 29, Young (Arsenal) 1.

Goals: (78) Robson 22, Dawes A 13, Barke 10, Gillespie 7, Smith J T 6, Blackman 4, Collins 3, Wilson 3, MacPhee 2, Geldard 1, Gregory M 1, Hawke1, Henley 1, Hudgell 1, Lewis G 1, Smith J F 1, own goal 1.

FULHAM

LONDON CUP 1940-41

Queen's Park Rangers (home) won 4-1 (Revell, Swinfen (og), Rooke, Keeping)
Hobbins; Hiles, Keeping, Evans, Cullis, Whittaker, Woodward, Robinson, Rooke, Taylor, Revell.

Queen's Park Rangers (away) won 7-4 (Rooke 4, Woodward, Evans, Robinson)
Hobbins; Hiles, Scaife, Evans, Griffiths R, Whittaker, McCormick, Robinson, Rooke, Woodward, Revell.

Crystal Palace (away) lost 5-2 (Revell, Beasley)
Hobbins; Hiles, Scaife, O'Leary, Griffiths R, Whittaker, Revell, Robinson, Rooke, Woodward, Beasley.

Brentford (home) won 4-1 (Revell, Rooke, Beasley, O'Callaghan)
Hobbins; Hiles, Howe, Evans, Cullis, Whittaker, Revell, Robinson, Rooke, O'Callaghan, Beasley.

Brentford (away) lost 7-4 (O'Callaghan 2, Keeping, Smith)
Hobbins; Hiles, Chalkley, O'Leary, Tompkins, Whittaker, Revell, Smith, Rooke, O'Callaghan, Keeping.

Crystal Palace (home) lost 4-1 (Robinson)
Hobbins; Hiles, Bacuzzi, Evans, Cullis, Whittaker, Mahon, Robinson, Woodward, O'Callaghan, Revell.

Aldershot (away) lost 3-1 (Trewick)
Hobbins; Scaife, Read, O'Leary, Hiles, Whittaker, Revell, Robinson, Rooke, Woodward, Trewick.

Aldershot (away) lost 4-2 (Rooke, Cullis)
Hobbins; Hiles, Bacuzzi, Matthewson, Cullis, O'Leary, Woodward, Robinson, Rooke, O'Callaghan, Revell.
(NB both Aldershot games at the Recreation Ground by arrangement)

Chelsea (home) 4-0 (Woodward 2, Rooke, O'Callaghan)
Joslin; Hiles, Bacuzzi, Matthewson, Cullis, Muttitt, Griffiths M, Woodward, Rooke, O'Callaghan, Revell.

Chelsea (away) lost 4-3 (Rooke 2, Woodward)
Hobbins; Hiles, Bacuzzi, Muttitt, Cullis, Tompkins, Revell, Woodward, Rooke, O'Callaghan, O'Leary.

Appearances: Bacuzzi 4, Beasley (Huddersfield) 2, Chalkley (West Ham) 1, Cullis (Wolves) 6, Evans 4, Griffiths R (Chelsea) 2, Griffiths M (Leicester) 1, Hiles 10, Hobbins (Charlton) 9, Howe (Spurs) 1, Joslin (Torquay) 1, Keeping 2, McCormick (Spurs) 1, Mahon (Huddersfield) 1, Matthewson (Bury) 2, Muttitt (Brentford) 2, O'Callaghan 6, O'Leary (Ipswich) 5, R Read 1, Revell (Charlton) 10, Robinson (Charlton) 7, Rooke 9, Scaife (Leeds) 3, Smith (Burnley) 1, Taylor 1, Tompkins 2, G Trewick 1, Whittaker (Charlton) 7, Woodward 8.

Goals: (32) Rooke 10, O'Callaghan 4, Woodward 4, Revell 3, Beasley 2, Keeping 2, Robinson 2, Cullis 1, Evans 1, Smith 1, Trewick 1, own goal 1.

LONDON LEAGUE 1941-42

Aldershot (home) lost 6-2 (Rooke 2 (1 pen))
Poland; Howe, Taylor, Muttitt, Cullis, Briggs F, Smith C, Walsh, Rooke, Milsom, Cranfield.

Millwall (away) won 4-2 (Rooke 2, Muttitt, Cranfield)
Joslin; Hiles, Malpass, Jones L, Cullis, Tompkins, Sibley, Muttitt, Rooke, Gallacher, Cranfield.

Arsenal (home) lost 5-2 (Rooke, Cranfield)
Joslin; Taylor, Malpass, Jones L, Hiles, Tompkins, Sibley, Muttitt, Rooke, Gallacher, Cranfield.

Queen's Park Rangers (away) won 5-2 (Rooke 4, Sibley)
Joslin; Freeman, Taylor, Jones L, Hiles, Tompkins, Sibley, Muttitt, Rooke, Gallacher, Cranfield.

Reading (home) drew 2-2 (Rooke 2)
Swift; Freeman, Taylor, Jones L, Cullis, Tompkins, Griffiths, Hiles, Rooke, Muttitt, Cranfield.

Brighton & Hove Albion (home) lost 3-2 (McCormick, Morgan)
Swift; Freeman, Malpass, Jones L, Hiles, Tompkins, Griffiths, McCormick, Rooke, Gallacher, Morgan.

Brentford (home) won 4-3 (Gallacher 2, Hiles 2)
Joslin; Freeman, Malpass, Jones L, Cullis, Tompkins, Jones E, Richardson, Hiles, Gallacher, Bonass.

Crystal Palace (away) lost 3-1 (Hiles)
Briggs C; Freeman, Malpass, Jones L, Cullis, Tompkins, Sibley, Richardson, Hiles, Gallacher, Cumner.

Clapton Orient (away) lost 2-1 (Jones E)
Swift; Hiles, Tompkins, Jones L, Tuckett, Ford, McCormick, Richardson, Rooke, Gallacher, Jones E.

Tottenham Hotspur (home) drew 2-2 (Rooke 2)
Swift; Bacuzzi, Freeman, Jones L, Cullis, Tompkins, Sibley, Richardson, Rooke, Gallacher, Jones E.

Portsmouth (away) l;ost 5-3 (Gallacher, Rooke, Richardson)
Duke; Freeman, Malpass, Jones L, Hiles, Lodge, Sibley, Richardson, Rooke, Gallacher, Jones E.

Chelsea (home) lost 4-1 (Freeman)
Hiles; Freeman, Scaife, Jones L, Matthewson, Tompkins, Sibley, Richardson, Rooke, Gallacher, Cumner.

Charlton Athletic (away) drew 3-3 (Rooke 2, Gallacher)
Duke; Hiles, Freeman, Jones L, Matthewson, Hamilton, Sibley, McCormick, Rooke, Gallacher, Bonass.

West Ham United (home) lost 3-1 (Jones L)
Duke; Hiles, Scaife, Jones L, Matthewson, Freeman, McCormick, Muttitt, Rooke, Gallacher, Bonass.

Watford (away) won 5-3 (Conley 2, Gallacher 2, Thomas)
Duke; Freeman, Kelly, Jones L, Matthewson, Pryde, Sibley, Jones E, Thomas, Gallacher, Conley.

Aldershot (away) lost 4-3 (Rooke 2 (1 pen), Rampling)
Duke; Freeman, Young, Jones L, Hiles, Pryde, Rampling, Skinner, Rooke, McCormick, Conley.

Millwall (home) won 4-3 (Rooke 4)
Duke; Mackie, Parry, Jones L, Hiles, Sneddon, Sibley, Rampling, Rooke, Gallacher, Conley.

Arsenal (away) lost 2-0
Duke; Hiles, Parry, Jones L, Matthewson, Freeman, Rampling, Dean, Rooke, Gallacher, Conley.

Queen's Park Rangers (home) lost 3-0
Duke; Bacuzzi, Hiles, Jones L, Matthewson, Freeman, Sibley, Rampling, Rooke, Gallacher, Conley.

Reading (away) lost 4-1 (Gallacher)
Duke; Bacuzzi, Whatley, Jones L, Hiles, Matthewson, Sibley, Rampling, Rooke, Gallacher, Conley.

Brighton & Hove Albion (away) won 7-3 (Rooke 2, Finch 2, Gallacher 2, Dean)
Duke; Hiles, Whatley, Whitfield, Matthewson, Tompkins, Finch, Dean, Rooke, Gallacher, Conley.

Brentford (away) won 3-2 (Dean 3)
Duke; Hiles, Whatley, Jones L, Matthewson, Whitfield, McCormick, Dean, Rooke, Gallacher, Conley.

Clapton Orient (home) won 5-1 (Conley 3, Dean, Finch)
Duke; Bacuzzi, Whatley, Jones L, Cullis, Hiles, Finch, Dean, Rooke, Gallacher, Conley.

Portsmouth (home) lost 7-2 (Conley 2)
Duke; Bacuzzi, Whatley, Jones L, Matthewson, Whitfield, Finch, Dean, Hiles, Gallacher, Conley.

Chelsea (away) won 5-1 (Rooke 2, Gallacher, Finch, Woodward)
Duke; Bacuzzi, Whatley, Evans, Matthewson, Whitfield, Woodward, Dean, Rooke, Gallacher, Finch.

Charlton Athletic (home) lost 7-4 (Dean 2, Rooke, Gallacher)
Duke; Bacuzzi, Whatley, Evans, Matrthewson, Hiles, Finch, Dean, Rooke, Gallacher, Conley.

West Ham United (away) drew 1-1 (Kiernan)
Duke; Whatley, Jones L, Evans, Cullis, Duffy, Finch, Kiernan, Rooke, Gallacher, Conley.

Watford (home) lost 3-1 (Finch)
Duke; Abel, Whatley, Duffy, Hiles, Whitfield, Finch, Nicholls, Neary, Thomas, Conley.

Tottenham Hotspur (away) lost 7-1 (Conley)
Duke; Bacuzzi, Marsden, Whitfield, Matthewson, Sharp, Foxall, Dean, Rooke, Gallacher, Cnnley.

Crystal Palace (home) won 4-3 (Conley 4)
Duke; Ward, Tickridge, Jones L, Matthewson, Thomas, Foxall, Dean, Gibbons, Finch, Conley.

LONDON CUP 1941-42

Portsmouth (away) lost 9-1 (Kiernan)
Duke; Malpass, Whatley, Duffy, Cullis, Keen, Finch, Dean, Ludford, Kiernan, Cranfield.

Chelsea (home) won 1-0 (Conley)
Duke; Bacuzzi, Compton L, Duffy, Matthewson, Keen, Finch, Kiernan, Dean, Gallacher, Conley.

Portsmouth (home) won 2-1 (Conley 2)
Duke; Smith E, Lester, Jones L, Matthewson, Duffy, Finch, Kiernan, Dean, Gallacher, Conley.

Chelsea (away) drew 2-2 (Conley 2)
Duke; Bacuzzi, Smith E, Jones L, Matthewson, Duffy, Foxall, Kiernan, Dean, Gallacher, Conley.

Crystal Palace (home) won 4-1 (Woodward 2, Conley, Gallacher)
Duke; Hiles, Wallbanks, Sharp, Matthewson, Holliday, Foxall, Dean, Woodward, Gallacher, Conley.

Crystal Palace (away) lost 5-4 (Rooke 3, Foxall)
Duke; Hiles, Buckingham, Sharp, Matthewson, Holliday, Foxall, Dean, Rooke, Gallacher, Conley.

Appearances: Abel (QPR) 1, Bacuzzi 10, Bonass (Chesterfield) 3, Briggs C (Halifax) 1, Briggs F (Wrexham) 1, Buckingham (Spurs) 1, Compton L (Arsenal) 1, Conley (Torquay) 20, Cranfield 6, Cullis (Wolves) 9, Cumner (Arsenal) 2, Dean (Southampton) 15, Duffy (Celtic) 6, Duke (Norwich) 25, Evans 3, Finch 11, Ford (Charlton) 1, Foxall (West Ham) 5, Freeman 14, Gallacher (Bournemouth) 30, A H Gibbons (Spurs) 1, Griffiths (Leicester) 2, Hamilton (St Bernards) 1, Hiles 25, Holliday (Brentford) 2, Howe (Spurs) 1, Jones E (WBA) 5, Jones L (Plymouth) 26, Joslin (Torquay) 4, Keen (Derby) 2, Kelly (Aldershot) 1, Kiernan (Albion R) 5, Lester (Sheff W) 1, Lodge (Huddersfield) 1, Ludford (Spurs) 1, McCormick (Spurs) 6, Mackie* 1, Malpass 7, Marsden (Bournemouth) 1, Matthewson (Bury) 19, Milsom J* 1, Morgan* (Arsenal) 1, Muttitt (Brentford) 6, H F Neary 1, E Nicholls 1, Parry (Ipswich) 2, Poland (Liverpool) 1, Pryde (Arsenal) 2, Rampling 5, Richardson (Millwall) 6, Rooke 25, Scaife (Leeds) 2, Sharp (Albion R) 3, Sibley (Southend) 12, Skinner (Spurs) 1, Smith C (Aberdeen) 1, Smith E (Millwall) 2, Sneddon (Swansea) 1, Swift (Man C) 4, Taylor (Wolves) 4, Thomas (Plymouth) 3, Tompkins 11, Tickridge (Spurs) 1, Tuckett 1, Wallbanks 1, Walsh (Millwall) 1, Ward (Spurs) 1, Whatley (Spurs) 10, Whitfield (Bristol R) 6, Woodward 2, Young (Arsenal) 1.

Goals: (93) Rooke 30, Conley 18, Gallacher 12, Dean 7, Finch 5, Hiles 3, Woodward 3, Cranfield 2, Kiernan 2, Foxall 1, Freeman 1, Jones E 1, Jones L 1, McCormick 1, Morgan 1, Muttitt 1, Rampling 1, Richardson 1, Sibley 1, Thomas 1.

MILLWALL

LONDON CUP 1940-41

West Ham United (home) lost 2-1 (Jinks)
Burke; Smith E, Williams, Dudley, Oakes, Forsyth, Voisey, Ross, Jinks, Lancelotte, Smith J R

West Ham United (away) lost 2-1 (Fisher)
Burke; Smith E, Williams, Dudley, Oakes, Forsyth, Fisher, Richardson, Jinks, Lancelotte, Smith J R.

Tottenham Hotspur (home) lost 3-1 (Forsyth)
Burke; Smith E, Williams, Dudley, Oakes, Forsyth, Fisher, Richardson, Jinks, Lancelotte, Smith J R.
Match played at White Hart Lane.

Tottenham Hotspur (away) lost 4-0
Burke; Smith E, Williams, Dudley, Oakes, Button, Fisher, Ross, Osborne G, Forsyth, Smith J R.

Reading (home) lost 2-0
Burke; Smith E, Williams, Dudley, Oakes, Forsyth, Fisher, Chapman, Davison, Grant, Smith J R.

Reading (away) drew 2-2 (Jinks, Dudley)
Burke; Tickridge, Wiliams, Hammond Forsyth, Ford, Fisher, Dudley, Jinks, Lancelotte, Smith J R

Clapton Orient (away) won 1-0 (Reid)
Burke; Tickridge, Williams, Ross, Smith E, Button, Fisher, Richardson, Forsyth, Reid, Smith J R

Arsenal; (home) lost 6-1 (Fisher)
Burke; Tickridge, Smith E, Ross, Forsyth, Dudley, Fisher, Richardson, Reid, Reeve, Smith J R.

Clapton Orient (home) won 4-0 (Reeve 3, Johnson)
Burke; Tickridge, Smith E, Forsyth, Chaney, Dudley, Pennington, Fisher, Johnson, Reeve, Smith J R.

Arsenal (home) lost 5-2 (Osborne J, Reid)
Burke; Tickridge, Smith E, Jobling, Bartlett, Button, Warnes, Reid, J Osborne, Smith J R, Mansfield.
(*NB both Arsenal games played at The Den*)

Appearances: Bartlett (C Orient) 1, Burke 10, R Button 3, F Chaney 1, Chapman* 1, Davison* 1, Dudley 8, Fisher 8, Ford (Charlton) 1, Forsyth 9, Grant* 1, Hammond (Charlton) 1, Jinks 4, Jobling (Charlton) 1, Johnson (Blackpool) 1, Lancelotte (Charlton) 4, Mansfield 1, John Oakes (Charlton), 5, G Osborne 1, J Osborne (Romford) 1, A Pennington 1, Reeve (Grimsby) 2, Reid (Norwich) 3, Richardson 4, Ross (Leith Ath) 4, Smith E 9, Smith J R 10, S Tickridge (Spurs) 5, Voisey W (Manager) 1, Warnes* 1, Williams 7.

Goals: (13) Reeve 3, Fisher 2, Jinks 2, Reid 2, Dudley l, Forsyth 1, Johnson 1, Osborne J 1.

LONDON LEAGUE 1941-42

Crystal Palace (away) lost 2-0
Burke; Dudley, Smith E, Reid, Sliman, Forsyth, Fisher, Needham, Jones F, Read, Smith J R.

Fulham (home) lost 4-2 (Richardson, Smith J R)
Burke; Calland, Smith E, Reid, Sliman, Forsyth, Fisher, Richardson, Jones F, Fenton, Smith J R.

Tottenham Hotspur (away) lost 3-0
Burke; Calland, Smith E, Reid, Sliman, Forsyth, Fisher, Richardson, Kilhourhy, Thomas, Dudley.

Portsmouth (home) lost 3-1 (Smith J R)
Burke; Calland, Smith E, Reid, Sliman, Forsyth, Fisher, Richardson, Kilhourhy, Beattie, Smith J R.

Chelsea (home) won 6-3 (Reid 2, Fisher, Bell, Smith J R, own goal)
Burke; Calland, Smith E, Malpass, Matthewson, Button, Fisher, Osborne, Reid, Bell, Smith J R.

Charlton Athletic (away) won 2-1 (Reid (pen), Bell)
Burke; Calland, Smith E, Forsyth, Matthewson, Dudley, Fisher, Osborne, Reid, Bell, Pattison.

West Ham United (away) lost 4-2 (Bell 2)
Burke; Calland, Smith E, Button, Forsyth, Muttitt, Fisher, Bell, Reid, Smith J R, Pattison.

Watford (home) won 4-2 (Fisher 3, Lawton)
Burke; Calland, Smith E, Dudley, Matthewson, Burrows, Fisher, Bell, Lawton, Smith J R, Pattison.

Aldershot (away) lost 5-2 (Osborne, Fisher)
Burke; Calland, Dudley, Brolly, Matthewson, Burrows, Fisher, Forsyth, Osborne, Bell, Mansfield.

Clapton Orient (home) drew 2-2 (Osborne 2)
Burke; Calland, Smith E, Forsyth, Gibson, Burrows, Fisher, Bell, Osborne, Smith J R, Osman.

Arsenal (home) drew 2-2 (Fisher, Bell)
Burke; Calland, Smith E, Sykes, Matthewson, Burrows, Fisher, Bell, Osborne, Forsyth, Osman.

Queen's Park Rangers (away) lost 4-1 (Bell)
Burke; Calland, Malpass, Forsyth, Cardwell, Dudley, Fisher, Bell, Gray, Smith J R, Osman.

Reading (away) lost 2-1 (Bell)
Burke; Calland, Dudley, Burrows, Cardwell, McClure, Vickers, Bell, Osborne, Gray, Smith J R.

Brighton & Hove Albion (away) lost 5-0
Burke; Calland, Smith E, Forsyth, Vickers, Preskett, Fisher, Gray, Croom, Bell, Burley.

Brentford (home) won 4-2 (Osborne 2, Bell, Mansfield)
Burke; Calland, Smith E, Dudley, Cardwell, Burrows, Fright, Bell, Osborne, Wright, Mansfield.

Crystal Palace (home) won 1-0 (Wright)
Burke; Calland, Smith E, Forsyth, Cardwell, Dudley, Fisher, Bell, Osborne, Wright, Mansfield.

Fulham (away) lost 4-3 (Bell, Osborne, Wright)
Burke; Smith E, Warboys, Forsyth, Cardwell, Burrows, Fisher, Bell, Osborne, Wright, Mansfield.

Tottenham Hotspur (home) lost 2-1 (Osborne)
Burke; Calland, Smith E, Forsyth, Dudley, Burrows, Fisher, Bell, Osborne, Johnson, Mansfield.

Portsmouth (away) lost 3-2 (Mansfield, Osborne)
Burke; Callland, Smith E, Burley, Dudley, Burrows, Fisher, Bell, Osborne, Wright, Mansfield.

Chelsea (away) drew 3-3 (Osborne 3)
Burke; Sproston, Smith E, Brown, Cardwell, Burrows, Fisher, Bell, Osborne, Wright, Mansfield.

Charlton Athletic (home) lost 1-0
Burke; Calland, Smith E, Forsyth, Brown, Cardwell, Fisher, Bell, Osborne, Groves, Burley.

West Ham United (home) lost 3-1 (Bell)
Burke; Dudley, Smith E, Butcher, Cardwell, Burrows, Fisher, Bell, Osborne, Groves, Burley.

Aldershot (home) won 3-1 (Bell 2, Smith E)
Burke; Scaife, Smith E, Butcher, Brown, Woodburn, Fisher, Bell, Morrison, Dudley, Burley.

Arsenal (away) lost 10-0
Burke; Scaife, Gray, Woodburn, McCabe, Butcher, Fisher, Bell, Anderson, Eastham, Burley.

Queen's Park Rangers (home) lost 2-1 (Eastham)
Burke; Scaife, Muir, Butcher, H Taylor, Burrows, Sibley, Bell, Gray, Eastham, Burley.

Reading (home) drew 1-1 (Fisher (pen))
Burke; Woodburn, Smith E, Forsyth, Cardwell, Burrows, Fisher, Richardson, Blackman, Bunce, Burley.

Brighton & Hove Albion (home) won 2-0 (Bell, Osborne)
Burke; Jones S, Smith E, Forsyth, Cardwell, Woodburn, Fisher, Bell, Osborne, Gillespie, Burley.

Brentford (away) lost 4-3 (Driver, Heathcote, own goal)
Purdie; Marsden, Jones S, Forsyth, Cardwell, Gray, Downer, Bell, Heathcote, Driver, Burley.

Clapton Orient (away) drew 3-3 (Heathcote, Dolding, Harrison)
Burke; O'Beirne, Scaife, Halton, Cardwell, Bell, Fisher, Dolding, Heathcote, Harrison, Burley.

Watford (away) lost 1-0
Purdie; Gray, Scaife, Bell, Halton, Harrison, Fisher, Dolding, Heathcote, Osborne, Birdseye.

LONDON CUP 1941-42

Queen's Park Rangers (home) drew 2-2 (Bell, Fisher)
Purdie; Scaife, Jones S, Packard, Gibson, Burrows, Fisher, Bell, Osborne, Driver, Burley,

Brentford (away) drew 3-3 (Sproston, Heathcote, Burrows)
Purdie; Scaife, Jones S, Packard, Cardwell, Burrows, Fisher, Halton, Heathcote, Sproston, Burley.

Aldershot (away) won 4-2 (Heathcote 2, Bell, Burley)
Purdie; Calland, Butler, Packard, Cardwell, Jones S, Fisher, Bell, Heathcote, Soo, Burley.

Brentford (home) drew 2-2 (Soo, Heathcote)
Purdie; Calland, Jones S, Marsden, Cardwell, Sproston, Fisher, Bell, Heathcote, Soo, Burley.

Aldershot (home) won 4-1 (Driver, Soo, Fisher, Heathcote)
Purdie; Calland, Taylor F, Halton, Packard, Burrows, Fisher, Driver, Heathcote, Soo, Burley.

Queen's Park Rangers (away) lost 2-0
Purdie; Calland, Scaife, Packard, Cardwell, Burrows, Fisher, Driver, Heathcote, Soo, Burley.

Appearances: Anderson (Bury) 1, Beattie 1, Bell (Southend) 28, F Birdseye 1, Blackman (C Palace) 1, Brolly 1, Brown (Hearts) 3, G Bunce 1, Burley (QPR) 17, Burke 28, Burrows (Sheff W) 17, Butcher (Chester) 4, Butler (Blackpool) 1, R Button 2, Calland (Torquay) 22, Cardwell (Man C) 16, Croom (Leeds) 1, L Dolding (QPR) 2, F Downer 1, Driver (Sheff W) 4, Dudley 13, Eastham (Blackpool) 2, Fenton 1, Fisher 32, Forsyth 18, E Fright (Short Spts) 1, S Gibson 2, Gillespie (C Palace) 1, Gray (Lincoln) 7, Groves (Stockport) 2, Halton (Bury) 4, I Harrison 2, Heathcote (QPR) 8, I Harrison 2, Johnson (Blackpool) 1, Jones F (Ipswich) 2, Jones S (Blackpool) 6, Killhourhy (Doncaster) 2, J Lawton 1, McCabe (Middlesbrough) 1, McClure (Kilmarnock) 1, Malpass (Fulham) 2, Mansfield 7, Marsden (Bournemouth) 2, Matthewson (Bury) 5, Morrison (Spurs) 1, Muir (Albion R) 1, Muttitt (Brentford) 1, Needham* 1, O'Beirne* 1, J Osborne (Romford) 17, Osman 3, Packard (Sheff W) 5, Pattison (QPR) 3, Preskett (Plymouth) 1, Purdie (Airdrie) 8, S Read 1, Reid (Stockport) 7, Richardson 4, Scaife (Leeds) 8, Sibley (Southend) 1, Sliman (Chelmsford) 4, Smith E 22, Smith J R 9, Soo (Stoke) 4, Sproston (Man C) 3, Sykes 1, Taylor F (Wolves) 1, H Taylor 1, Thomas (Plymouth) 1, Vickers* 2, G Warboys 1, Woodburn (Newcastle) 4, Wright (Chelmsford) 5.

Goals: (68) Bell 15, Osborne 12, Fisher 9, Heathcote 7, Reid 3, Smith J R 3, Driver 2, Mansfield 2, Soo 2, Wright 2, Burley 1, Burrows 1, Dolding 1, Eastham 1, Harrison 1, Lawton 1, Richardson 1, Smith E 1, Sproston 1, own goals 2.

PORTSMOUTH

LONDON LEAGUE 1941-42

West Ham United (away) won 3-1 (Black 2, Barlow)
Walker; Morgan, Rochford, Guthrie, Flewin, Summerbee, McIntosh, Black, Moores, Barlow, Parker.

Watford (away) won 5-1 (Barlow 3, Black 2)
Walker; Morgan, Rochford, Guthrie, Flewin, McIntosh, Emery, Black, Moores, Barlow, Parker.

Aldershot (home) drew 2-2 (Parker, Black)
Walker; Morgan, Rochford, Guthrie, Flewin, Summerbee, McIntosh, Black, Moores, Barlow, Parker.
Match abandoned 77 minutes; broken goal post.

Millwall (away) won 3-1 (Black 2, Moores)
Walker; Morgan, Rochford, Guthrie, Flewin, Summerbee, McIntosh, Black, Moores, Barlow, Parker.

Arsenal (home) lost 5-1 (Guthrie)
Walker; Morgan, Rochford, Guthrie, Flewin, Summerbee, McIntosh, Black, Moores, Barlow, Parker.

Queen's Park Rangers (away) won 2-0 (Black 2)
Walker; Morgan, Rochford, Guthrie, Flewin, Summerbee, Aston, Ward, Moores, Black, Parker.

Reading (home) won 1-0 (Moores)
Walker; Morgan, Rochford, Guthrie, Flewin, Summerbee, Aston, Black, Moores, Barlow, Parker.

Brighton & Hove Albion (away) lost 2-1 (McIntosh)
Walker; Morgan, Rochford, Guthrie, Flewin, Summerbee, Aston, Black, McIntosh, Barlow, Parker.

Brentford (home) won 2-1 (Parker, Rochford)
Walker; Morgan, Rochford, Guthrie, Flewin, Wharton, McIntosh, Black, Ward, Barlow, Parker.

Crystal Palace (away) lost 3-1 (Black)
Walker; Morgan, Rochford, Guthrie, Flewin, Summerbee, McIntosh, Black, Ward, Barlow, Parker.

Fulham (home) won 5-3 (Black 2, Ward 2, Parker)
Walker; Morgan, Rochford,, Guthrie, Flewin, Wharton, McIntosh, Black, Ward, Barlow, Parker.

Tottenham Hotspur (home) lost 2-1 (Black)
Platt; Morgan, Rochford, Guthrie, Flewin, Summerbee, Harrigan, Black, Ward, Barlow, Parker.

Clapton Orient (away) won 4-0 (Moores, Ward, Aston, Barnes (og))
Walker; Morgan, Rochford, Guthrie, Flewin, Wharton, Ward, Aston, Moores, Barlow, Parker.

Chelsea (home) lost 3-2 (Moores, Black)
Walker; Morgan, Rochford, Guthrie, Flewin, Summerbee, Ward, Black, Moores, Barlow, Parker.

Charlton Athletic (home) won 7-2 (Black 4, Griffiths 2, Barlow)
Walker; Morgan, Rochford, Guthrie, Flewin, Summerbee, Worrall, Griffiths, Black, Barlow, Parker.

West Ham United (home) won 1-0 (Black)
Walker; Morgan, Rochford, Guthrie, Slater, Summerbee, Ward, Griffiths, Black, Barlow, Parker.

Watford (home) won 7-1 (Black 3, Barlow 2, Griffiths 2)
Walker; Morgan, Rochford, Guthrie, Slater, Summerbee, Ward, Griffiths, Black, Barlow, Parker.

Aldershot (away) lost 3-2 (Emery, Guthrie (pen))
Walker; Morgan, Rochford, Gregory, Flewin, Guthrie, Emery, Griffiths, Ward, Black, Parker.

Millwall (home) won 3-2 (Black 2, Guthrie (pen))
Walker; Morgan, Rochford, Gregory, Guthrie, Summerbee, Emery, Griffiths, Ward, Black, Parker.

Arsenal (away) lost 6-1 (Barlow)
Walker; Burke, Rochford, Ward, Flewin, Guthrie, Emery, Griffiths, Moores, Barlow, Parker.

Queen's Park Rangers (home) won 3-1 (Black, Ward, Griffiiths)
Ranner; Morgan, Rochford, Guthrie, Flewin, Wharton, Emery, Griffiths, Black, Barlow, Ward.

Reading (away) lost 5-2 (Moores, Barlow)
Walker; Morgan, Burke, Guthrie, Flewin, Summerbee, Ward, Griffiths, Moores, Barlow, Parker.

Brighton & Hove Albion (home) won 5-3 (Black 2, Guthrie (pen), Barlow, Risdon (og))
Walker; Morgan, Rochford, Guthrie, Flewin, Wharton, Emery, Griffiths, Black, Barlow, Parker.

Brentford (away) won 5-2 (Black 2, Barlow 2, Griffiths)
Walker; Morgan, Rochford, Sykes, Flewin, Summerbee, Emery, Griffiths, Black, Barlow, Parker.

Crystal Palace (home) won 3-1 (Court 3)
Walker; Morgan, Rochford, Guthrie, Flewin, Summerbee, Bullock, Griffiths, Court, Barlow, Parker.

Fulham (away) won 7-2 (Barlow 3, Bullock 2, Griffiths, Parker)
Walker; Morgan, Rochford, Guthrie, Flewin, Summerbee, Bullock, Griffiths, Court, Barlow, Parker.

Tottenham Hotspur (away) drew 1-1 (Griffiths)
Walker; Morgan, Rochford, Guthrie, Flewin, Summerbee, Griffiths, Martin, Wharton, Barlow, Parker.

Clapton Orient (home) won 16-1 (Black 8, Griffiths 2, Barlow 2, Parker 2, Guthrie, Bullock)
Walker; Morgan, Rochford, Guthrie, Flewin, Summerbee, Bullock, Griffiths, Black, Barlow, Parker.

Chelsea (away won 4-3 (Black 2, Barlow, Compton L (og))
Walker; Morgan, Rochford, Guthrie, Flewin, Summerbee, Bullock, Griffiths, Black, Barlow, Parker.

Charlton Athletic (away) won 5-2 (Black 2, Barlow 2, Moores)
Walker; Morgan, Rochford, Guthrie, Flewin, Summerbee, Moores, Ward, Black, Barlow, Parker.

LONDON CUP 1941-42

Fulham (home) won 9-1 (Barlow 3, Griffiths 3, Bullock 2, Moores)
Walker; Morgan, Rochford, Guthrie, Flewin, Summerbee, Bullock, Griffiths, Moores, Barlow, Parker.

Crystal Palace (away) won 2-0 (Griffiths, Bullock)
Walker; Morgan, Rochford, Guthrie, Flewin, Wharton, Bullock, Griffiths, Black, Barlow, Parker.

Fulham (away) lost 2-1 (Moores)
Walker; Morgan, Rochford, Guthrie, Flewin, Summerbee, Bullock, Griffiths, Moores, Barlow, Parker.

Crystal Palace (home) won 2-1 (Black 2)
Walker; Rookes, Rochford, Guthrie, Flewin, Whartoh, Ward, Griffiths, Black, Barlow, Parker.

Chelsea (home) won 2-0 (Black 2)
Walker; Rookes, Rochfofd, Guthrie, Flewin, Summerbee, Bullock, Griffiths, Black, Barlow, Laney.

Chelsea (away) drew 0-0
Walker; Rookes, Rochford, Guthrie, Flewin, Wharton, Bullock, Griffiths, Black, Barlow, Parker.

Charlton Athletic (semi-final away at Stamford Bridge) won 1-0 (Black)
Walker; Rookes, Rochford, Guthrie, Flewin, Wharton, Bullock, Griffiths, Black, Barlow, Parker.

Brentford (final at Wembley) lost 2-0
Walker; Rookes, Rochford, Guthrie, Flewin, Wharton, Bullock, Griffiths, Black, Barlow, Parker.

Appearances: Aston (Man U) 4, Barlow 35, Black (Hearts) 30, Bullock (Barnsley) 11, Burke (Blackpool) 2, Court (Cardiff) 2, Emery 7, Flewin 35, Gregory M (C Palace) 2, Griffiths 23, Guthrie 37, Harrigan (St Mirren) 1, Laney (Southampton) 1, Martin (Villa) 1, McIntosh (Preston) 9, P Moores 14, Morgan 32, Parker 36, Platt (Arsenal) 1, Ranner (Royal Marines) 1, Rochford 37, Rookes 5, Slater (Rochdale) 2, Summerbee (Preston) 25, Sykes (Millwall) 1, Walker 36, Ward (Sheff W) 16, Wharton 11, Worrall 1.

Goals: (123) Black 47, Barlow 23, Griffiths 14, Moores 8, Bullock 6, Parker 6, Guthrie 5, Ward 4, Court 3, Aston 1, Emery 1, McIntosh 1, Rochford 1, own goals 3.

QUEEN'S PARK RANGERS

LONDON CUP 1940-41

Fulham (away) lost 4-1 (Mangnall)
Mason; Swinfen, Abel, March, Ridyard, Farmer, Webb, Lowe, Mangnall, Bott, Bonass.

Fulham (home) lost 7-5 (Lowe, March, Bonass, Bott, Mangnall)
Mason; Swinfen, Abel, March, Ridyard, Farmer, Webb, Lowe, Mangnall, Bott, Bonass.

Aldershot (home) lost 3-2 (Mallett 2)
Allen; Swinfen, Mortimer, Lowe, Ridyard, March, Webb, Mallett, Bott, Bonass, Pattison.

Chelsea (home) won 5-2 (Lowe, Mangnall, McEwan 2, Bott)
Mason; Abel, Jefferson, Swinfen, Ridyard, March, Webb, McEwan, Mangnall, Lowe, Bott.

Aldershot (away) won 4-2 (Mangnall, Daniels, Adam, March)
Mason; Swinfen, Abel, March, Ridyard, Farmer, Hillard, Lowe, Mangnall, Daniels, Adam.

Crystal Palace (away) won 2-1 (Mangnall, Fitzgerald)
Mason; Abel, Edwards, March, Ridyard, Farmer, Webb, Lowe, Mangnall, Fitzgerald, Halford.

Brentford (away) lost 4-2 (Mangnall 2)
Mason; Abel, Farmer, March, Ridyard, Armstrong, Webb, Lowe, Mangnall, Fitzgerald, Edwards.

Crystal Palace (home) won 2-1 (Davie 2)
Mason; Reay, Abel, March, Ridyard, Farmer, Webb, Lowe, Davie, Fitzgerald, Halford.

Brentford (home) drew 0-0
Mason; Reay, Jefferson, March, Ridyard, Farmer, Webb, Mangnall, Davie, Lowe, Adam.

Chelsea (away) won 3-2 (Mangnall 2, Davie)
Mason; Reay, Jefferson, March, Ridyard, Farmer, Lowe, Mangnall, Davie, Halford, Adam.

Appearances: Abel 7, Adam (Leicester) 3, Allen 1, Armstrong (Bristol C) 1, Bonass 3, Bott 4, H Daniels 1, Davie (Brighton) 3, E Edwards 2, Farmer 8, Fitzgerald 3, Halford (Oldham) 3, Hillard* 1, Jefferson 3, Lowe 10, Mallett 1, Mangnall 8, March 10, Mason 9, McEwan 1, Mortimer* 1, Pattison 1, Reay 3, Ridyard 10, Swinfen 5, J Webb 8.

Goals: (26) Mangnall 9, Davie 3, Bott 2, Lowe 2, McEwan 2, Mallett 2, March 2, Adam 1, Bonass 1, Daniels 1, Fitzgerald 1.

LONDON LEAGUE 1941-42 – RESULTS - APPEARANCES AND GOALS

Brighton & Hove Albion (away) won 5-2 (Davie 3, Mahon, Pattison)
Mason; Abel, Farmer, Lowe, Ridyard, March, Mahon, Mangnall, Davie, Armstrong, Pattison.

Brentford (home) lost 4-3 (Mallett, Halford, Mahon)
Mason; Swinfen, Abel, Lowe, Ridyard, March, Mahon, Eastham, Mangnall, Mallett, Halford.

Crystal Palace (away) lost 2-1 (Halford)
Mason; Abel, E Edwards, March, Ridyard, Farmer, Mahon, Lowe, Mangnal, R Edwards, Halford.

Fulham (home) lost 5-2 (Eastham 2)
Mason; Abel, Jefferson, March, Ridyard, Farmer, Mangnall, Eastham, Paton, Mallett, Halford.

Tottenham Hotspur (away) lost 3-1 (Mangnall)
Mason; Abel, Jefferson, Campbell, Ridyard, Farmer, Mangnall, Paton, Davie, Mallett, Pattison.

Portsmouth (home) lost 2-0
Mason; Swinfen, Jefferson, March, Ridyard, Farmer, Mahon, Paton, Mangnall, Eastham, Halford.

Chelsea (home) won 2-1 (Mahon, Mallett)
Mason; Abel, Farmer, Campbell, Ridyard, March, Mangnall, Eastham, Kirkham, Mallett, Mahon.

Charlton Athletic (home) drew 0-0
Mason; Abel, Jefferson, Campbell, Ridyard, March, Mangnall, Eastham, Kirkham, Mallett, Halford.

West Ham United (away) lost 2-0
Mason; Abel, Farmer, Campbell, Ridyard, March, Mangnall, Eastham, Kirkham, Mallett, Halford.

Watford (home) lost 5-1 (Pattison)
Mason; Swinfen, Abel, Campbell, Ridyard, March, Mahon, Eastham, Kirkham, Mangnall, Pattison.

Aldershot (away) lost 4-1 (Pattison)
Mason; Abel, Jefferson, Mallett, Mangnall, Blizzard, Mahon, Painter, Kirkham, Eastham, Pattison.

Millwall (home) won 4-1 (Stock 2, Mahon, Pattison)
Brown H; Abel, March, Mallett, Riidyard, Blizzard, Mangnall, Kirkham, Stock, Mahon, Pattison.

Arsenal (away) lost 4-1 (Pattison)
Brown H; Abel, Jefferson, March, Ridyard, Blizzard, Mangnall, Kirkham, Stock, Mahon, Pattison.

Clapton Orient (away) drew 0-0
Mason; Abel, Farmer, Blizzard, Ridyard, E Edwards, Mahon, Painter, Mangnall, Smale, Pattison.

Reading (away) drew 2-2 (Armstrong, Kirkham)
Mason; Abel, Jefferson, Mallett, Farmer, Blizzard, McEwan, Kirkham, Stock, Armstrong, Pattison.

Brighton & Hove Albion (home) won 3-0 (Mangnall 2, Armstrong)
Brown H; Swinfen, McNickle, Farmer, Ridyard, Blizzard, Mahon, Armstrong, Ling, Mangnall, Pattison.

Brentford (away) lost 4-3 (Mangnall 2, Abel)
Mason; Swinfen, Jefferson, Farmer, Ridyard, Blizzard, Abel, Mallett, Kirkham, Mangnall, Pattison.

Crystal Palace (home) lost 3-1 (Harris)
Mason; Swinfen, Dale, Farmer, Ridyard, Blizzard, Cottam, Armstrong, Harris, Mangnall, Bonass.

Fulham (away) won 3-0 (Moore, Mangnall, own goal)
Mason; Swinfen, Painter, Farmer, Ridyard, Blizzard, Lowe, Mallett, J Moore, Mangnall, Bonass.

Tottenham Hotspur (home) won 1-0 (Mallett)
Brown H; Abel, March, Farmer, Ridyard, Blizzard, Bonass, Mallett, Armstrong, Mangnall, Mahon.

Portsmouth (away) lost 3-1 (Mangnall)
Brown H; Abel, Farmer, Libby, Ridyard, Blizzard, Mahon, Bonass, Armstrong, Mangnall, Pattison.

Chelsea (away) lost 3-1 (Mangnall)
Brown H; Reay, Jefferson, Mallett, Ridyard, Blizzard, Mahon, Smith, Stock, Mangnall, Pattison.

Charlton Athletic (away) lost 3-1 (Mangnall)
Brown H; Reay, Farmer, Mallett, Ridyard, Blizzard, Lowe, Armstrong, Stock, Mangnall, Pattison.

West Ham United (home) won 2-1 (Armstrong, Farmer)
Brown H; Reay, Jefferson, Mallett, Ridyard, Farmer, Lowe, Armstrong, Kirkham, Mangnall, March.

Aldershot (home) lost 2-0
Mason; Reay, Jefferson, Mallett, Ridyard, Farmer, Swinfen, Smith, Mangnall, Hatton, Pattison.

Millwall (away) won 2-1 (Hatton 2)
Mason; Reay, Jefferson, Hatton, Ridyard, Farmer, Lowe, Smith, Heath, Armstrong, Pattison.

Arsenal (home) lost 1-0
Brown H; Lowe, Jefferson, Mallett, Ridyard, Farmer, Mangnall, Smith, Kirkham, Hatton, Pattison.

Clapton Orient (home) won 2-1 (Hatton, Mangnall)
Brown H; Lowe, Abel, Armstrong, Farmer, Blizzard, Sibley, Mangnall, Heath, Hatton, Pattison.

Reading (home) won 4-0 (Hatton 2, Mangnall 2)
Mason; Reay, Jefferson, Lowe, Ridyard, Farmer, Sibley, Mangnall, Kirkham, Hatton, Heath.

Watford (away) won 5-0 (Heath 2, McEwan 2, Lowe)
Brown H; Swinfen, Jefferson, Gunner, Ridyard, Mallett, Sibley, Lowe, McEwan, Smith, Heath.

LONDON CUP 1941-42

Millwall (away) drew 2-2 (Hatton 2)
Mason; Reay, Jefferson, Lowe, Farmer, Smith, Sibley, Mangnall, Kirkham, Hatton, Pattison.

Aldershot (away) won 2-0 (Kirkham, Hatton)
Mason; Reay, Jefferson, Swinfen, Ridyard, Farmer, Sibley, Mallett, Kirkham, Hatton, Heath.

Brentford (home) lost 2-1 (Kirkham)
Mason; Abel, Jefferson, Gunner, Ridyard, Farmer, Sibley, Armstrong, Kirkham, Hatton, Bonass.

Aldershot (home) lost 2-1 (Lowe)
Mason; Delaney, Abel, Gunner, Ridyard, March, B Brown, Lowe, Gibbs-Kennett, Farmer, Bonass.

Brentford (away) lost 1-0
Brown H; Reay, Jefferson, Gunner, Ridyard, Smith, Sibley, Mallett, Swinfen, McEwan, Heath.

Millwall (home) won 2-0 (Hatton 2)
Brown H; Swinfen, Jefferson, Mallett, Ridyard, Smith, Sibley, McEwan, Cheetham, Hatton, Bonass.

Appearances: Abel 20, Armstrong (Bristol C) 11, Blizzard 14, Bonass 7, B Brown 1, Brown H 13, Campbell* 5, Cheetham (Brentford) 1, Cottam* 1, Dale (Portsmouth) 1, Davie (Brighton) 2, Delaney (Arsenal) 1, Eastham (Blackpool) 8, E Edwards 2, R Edwards 1, Farmer 26, R Gibbs-Kennett 1, R Gunner 4, Halford (Oldham) 6, N Harris (Swansea) 1, Hatton (Notts Co) 9, W Heath 6, Jefferson 20, Kirkham (Bournemouth) 15, J Libby 1, L Ling 1, Lowe 13, Mahon (Huddersfield) 14, Mallett 21, Mangnall 28, March 14, Mason 23, McEwan 4, McNickle (Linfield) 1, J Moore 1, Painter (Swindon) 3, Paton (Bournemouth) 3, Pattison 18, Reay 9, Ridyard 32, Sibley (Southend) 8, Smale (Chelsea) 1, Smith 8, Stock 5, Swinfen 12.

Goals: (60) Mangnall 12, Hatton 10, Pattison 5, Mahon 4, Armstrong 3, Davie 3, Kirkham 3, Mallett 3, Eastham 2, Halford 2, Heath 2, Lowe 2, McEwan 2, Stock 2, Abel 1, Farmer 1, Harris 1, Moore 1, own goal 1.

READING

LONDON CUP 1940-41

Arsenal (home) won 2-0 (Edelston, MacPhee)
Mapson; Bacuzzi, Fullwood, Dougall, Ratcliffe, Layton, Chitty, Edelston, MacPhee, McColl, Sherwood.

Arsenal (away) won 1-0 (Cothliff)
Mapson; Chitty, Fullwood, Dougall, Ratcliffe, Layton, Tait, Cothliff, MacPhee, Collingham, Brooks.

Clapton Orient (away) won 4-0 (Cothliff, Edelston 2, MacPhee)
Mapson; Westwood, Fullwood, Dougall, Ratcliffe, Layton, Chitty, Edelston, MacPhee, Cothliff, Sherwood.

Millwall (away) won 2-0 (Brooks, MacPhee)
Swift; Glidden, Fullwood, Dougall, Ratcliffe, Layton, Chitty, Edelston, MacPhee, Cothliff, Brooks.

Millwall (home) drew 2-2 (Layton (pen), Sherwood)
Penny; McPhie, Westwood, Dougall, Ratcliffe, Layton, Chitty, Cothliff, MacPhee, McColl, Sherwood.

West Ham United (away) drew 1-1 (MacPhee)
Mapson; Chitty, Fullwood, Young, Ratcliffe, Layton, Sherwood, Wilkins, MacPhee, Cothliff, Warburton.

Clapton Orient (home) won 9-0 (MacPhee 4, Deverall, Bradley 2, Chitty, Brooks)
Mapson; McPhie, Fullwood, Cothliff, Ratcliffe, Layton, Chitty, Deverall, MacPhee, Bradley, Brooks.

West Ham United (home) won 4-1 (Layton, Cothliff, MacPhee 2)
Mapson; McPhie, Fullwood, Young, Ratcliffe, Layton, Hopper, Cothliff, MacPhee, Sherwood, Chitty.

Tottenham Hotspur (away) drew 2-2 (MacPhee, Chitty)
Mapson; McPhie, Fullwood, Cothliff, Ratcliffe, Layton, Chitty, Edelston, MacPhee, Eastham, Oxberry.

Tottenham Hotspur (home) drew 2-2 (MacPhee, Layton)
Mapson; Chitty, Fullwood, Cothliff, McPhie, Layton, Ireland, Bradley, MacPhee, Eastham, Brooks.

Crystal Palace (semi-final home) won 4-1 (MacPhee 3, Edelston)
Mapson; McPhie, Fullwood, Young, Ratcliffe, Layton, Chitty, Edelston, MacPhee, Bradley, Sherwood.

Brentford (final home) won 3-2 (Sherwood, Chitty, Edelston)
Mapson; McPhie, Fullwood, Young, Ratcliffe, Layton, Chitty, Edelston, MacPhee, Bradley, Sherwood.

Appearances: Bacuzzi (Fulham) 1, Bradley (Southampton) 4, N Brooks 4, Chitty 12, Collingham* 1, Cothliff (Torquay) 9, Deverall 1, Dougall 5, Eastham (Blackpool) 2, M Edelston 6, Fullwood 11, Glidden 1, A Hopper 1, H Ireland 1, Layton 12, MacPhee 12, McColl* 2, McPhie (Falkirk) 7, Mapson (Sunderland) 10, Oxberry (Trainer) 1, H Penny 1, Ratcliffe (Oldham)11, Sherwood 7, Swift (Man C) 1, Tait (Torquay) 1, Warburton (Chester) 1, Westwood (Man C) 2, Wilkins (Brentford) 1, Young 4.

Goals: (36) MacPhee 15, Edelston 5, Chitty 3, Cothliff 3, Layton 3, Bradley 2, Brooks 2, Sherwood 2, Deverall 1.

LONDON LEAGUE 1941-42

Clapton Orient (away) won 8-3 (Edelston 3, Bradley 2, Chitty, MacPhee, Sherwood)
Mapson; McPhie, Fullwood, Cothliff, Ratcliffe, Layton, Chitty, Edelston, MacPhee, Bradley, Sherwood.

Brighton & Hove Albion (home) lost 5-4 (MacPhee 2, Chitty, Cothliff)
Mapson; McPhie, Fullwood, Young, Ratcliffe, Layton, Chitty, Edelston, MacPhee, Cothliff, Duns.

Brentford (away) lost 3-2 (Deverall 2)
Mapson; McPhie, Fullwood, Young, Ratcliffe, Layton, Duns, Cothliff, MacPhee, Deverall, Chitty.

Crystal Palace (home) won 6-2 (MacPhee 5, Chitty)
Mapson; Goldberg, Fullwood, Young, Ratcliffe, Layton, Chitty, Hall, MacPhee, Cothliff, Sherwood.

Fulham (away) drew 2-2 (Edelston, MacPhee)
Mapson; Goldberg, Fullwood, Young, Ratclifffe, Layton, Duns, Cothliff, MacPhee, Edelston, Chitty.

Tottenham Hotspur (home) drew 1-1 (Bradley)
Mapson; Goldberg, Fullwood, Cothliff, Ratcliffe, Layton, Duns, Sherwood, MacPhee, Bradley, Chitty.

Portsmouth (away) lost 1-0
Mapson; McPhie, Fullwood, Young, Ratcliffe, Layton, Duns, Cothliff, MacPhee, Edelston, Chitty.

Chelsea (away) won 5-0 (Edelston 3, MacPhee, Bradley)
Mapson; McPhie, Fullwood, Young, Ratcliffe, Layton, Duns, Edelston, MacPhee, Bradley, Chitty.

Charlton Athletic (away) won 3-2 (Bradley 2 (1 pen), MacPhee)
Mapson; Goldberg, Fullwood, McPhie, Ratcliffe, Young, Duns, Cothliff, MacPhee, Bradley, Chitty.

West Ham United (home) won 3-2 (Cothliff 2, Chitty)
Mapson; Goldberg, Fullwood, McPhie, Ratcliffe, Young, Duns, Edelston, MacPhee, Cothliff, Chitty.

Watford (away) drew 0-0
Mapson; McPhie, Fullwood, Cothliff, Ratcliffe, Young, Chitty, Edwards, MacPhee, Court, Beasley.

Aldershot (home) drew 3-3 (Chitty 2, MacPhee)
Mapson; McPhie, Fullwood, Cothliff, Ratcliffe, Young, Chitty, Edelston, MacPhee, Bradley, Duns;

Millwall (home) won 2-1 (MacPhee, Beasley)
Davison; McPhie, Fullwood, Young, Ratcliffe, Wright, Chitty, Cothliff, MacPhee, Beasley, Brooks.

Arsenal (away) lost 3-1 (MacPhee)
Mapson; Wilson, Fullwood, Cothliff, Ratcliffe, Layton, Chitty, Edelston, MacPhee, Taylor, Court.

Queen's Park Rangers (home) drew 2-2 (MacPhee, Taylor)
Mapson; McPhie, Fullwood, Cook, Ratcliffe, Young, Chitty, Taylor, MacPhee, Bradley, Beasley.

Clapton Orient (home) won 2-0 (Edelston 2)
Mapson; McPhie, Chitty, Young, Ratcliffe, Wright, Sanders, Edelston, MacPhee, Cothliff, Court.

Brighton & Hove Albion (away) won 5-1 (Edelston 3, MacPhee, Chitty)
Mapson; McPhie, Fullwood, Young, Ratcliffe, Layton, Chitty, Edelston, MacPhee, Cothliff, Beasley.

Brentford (home) won 4-3 (Cothliff 2, MacPhee, Davie)
Mapson; Goldberg, Fullwood, Allum, Ratcliffe, Young, Chitty, Edelston, MacPhee, Cothliff, Davie.

Crystal Palace (away) drew 1-1 (Court)
Mapson; Chitty, Fullwood, Cothliff, Ratcliffe, McPhie, Sanders, Edelston, MacPhee, Court, Chapman.

Fulham (home) won 4-1 (MaxPhee 2, Edelston, Hall)
Mapson; McPhie, Fullwood, Young, Ratcliffe, Wright, Chitty, Edelston, MacPhee, Hall, Beasley.

Tottenham Hotspur (away) lost 2- 1 (Chitty)
Mapson; Goldberg, Fullwood, Young, Ratcliffe, Cothliff, Chitty, Hall, MacPhee, Taylor, Hopper.

Portsmouth (home) won 5-2 (Bradley 4, Cothliff)
Mapson; Chitty, Fullwood, Howe, Ratcliffe, Young, Cothliff, Deverall, MacPhee, Bradley, Court.

Charlton Athletic (home) lost 4-1 (Edelston)
Mapson; McPhie, Fullwood, Howe, Ratcliffe, Young, Chitty, Edelston, MacPhee, Cothliff, Beasley.

Watford (home) won 5-1 (MacPhee 2, Edelston 2, Bradley)
Mapson; McPhie, Fullwood, Howe, Ratcliffe, Cothliff, Chitty, Edelston, MacPhee, Bradley, Beasley.

Aldershot (away) drew 0-0
Mapson; McPhie, Fullwood, Howe, Ratcliffe, Cothliff, Chitty, Edelston, MacPhee, Hopper, Court.

Millwall (away) drew 1-1 (MacPhee)
Mapson; Goldberg, Fullwood, Howe, Ratcliffe, Cothliff, Chitty, Edelston, MacPhee, Stephenson, Beasley.

Arsenal (home) lost 4-1 (Stephenson)
Mapson; Goldberg, Fullwood, Howe, Ratcliffe, Cothliff, Chitty, Edelston, MacPhee, Stephenson, Bradley.

Queen's Park Rangers (away) lost 4-0
Mapson; Chitty, Fullwood, Young, Ratcliffe, Layton, Hopper, Howe, MacPhee, Cothliff, Beasley.

West Ham United (away) lost 2-1 (Cothliff)
Mapson; Goldberg, Muttitt, Tennant, Fullwood, Layton, Chitty, Taylor, Cothliff, Deverall, Oxberry.

Chelsea (home) won 3-2 (Bradley 2, Edelston)
Mapson; Goldberg, Burchell, Henley, Fullwood, Cothliff, Chitty, Edelston, MacPhee, Bradley, Deverall.

LONDON CUP 1941-42

Tottenham Hotspur (home) lost 2-1 (Edelston)
Davison; Goldberg, Ratcliffe, Cothliff, Young, Layton, Chitty, Edelston, MacPhee, Bradley, Court.

Charlton Athletic (away) drew 1-1 (Beasley)
Mapson; Goldberg, Chitty, Young, Ratcliffe, Layton, Cothliff, Henley, Court, Bradley, Beasley.

Tottenham Hotspur (away) lost 2-1 (MacPhee)
Mapson; McPhie, Fullwood, Young, Ratcliffe, Layton, Chitty, Hall, MacPhee, Bradley, Beasley.

Charlton Athletic (home) lost 5-3 (Henley 3)
Mapson; McPhie, Fullwood, Cothliff, Ratcliffe, Layton, Chitty, Edelston, MacPhee, Henley, Beasley.

Watford (away) lost 6-0
Mapson; Chitty, Fullwood, Cothliff, McPhie, Layton, Hopper, Edelston, MacPhee, Lane, Court.

Watford (home) won 3-0 (Henley, Bradley, Cothliff)
Mapson; Goldberg, Fullwood, McPhie, Ratcliffe, Layton, Chitty, Henley, Cothliff, Bradley, Hopper.

Appearances: Allum (C Orient) 1, Beasley (Huddersfield) 12, Bradley (Southampton) 14, N Brooks 1, G Burchell (Romford) 1, Chapman* 1, Chitty 36, Cook* 1, Cothliff (Torquay) 32, Court (Cardiff) 9, Davison (Blackburn) 2, Davie (Brighton) 1, Deverall 4, Duns (Sunderland) 9, M Edelston 22, Edwards 1, Fullwood 33, Goldberg (Leeds) 14, Hall A (Spurs) 4, Henley (Arsenal) 4, A Hopper 5, Howe (Spurs), 7, Lane (ex-Orient) 1, Layton 18, MacPhee 33, Mapson (Sunderland) 34, McPhie 22, Muttitt (Brentford) 1, Oxberry (Trainer) 1, Ratcliffe (Oldham) 33, Sanders* 2, Sherwood 3, Stephenson (Leeds) 2, Taylor 4, Tennant (Chelsea) 1, Wilson 1, Wright (Charlton) 3, Young 23.

Goals: (85) MacPhee 23, Edelston 18, Bradley 14, Chitty 8, Cothliff 8, Henley 4, Beasley 2, Deverall 2, Court 1, Davie 1, Hall 1, Sherwood 1, Stephenson 1, Taylor 1.

TOTTENHAM HOTSPUR

LONDON CUP 1940-41

Clapton Orient (home) won 3-0 (Gibbons 3)
Hooper; Ward, Whatley, White, Hitchins, Hall G W, O'Callaghan, Broadis, Gibbons, Duncan, Ludford.

Clapton Orient (away) won 9-1 (Hall, Duncan, Gibbons 3, Broadis 2, Ludford 2)
Hooper; Ward, Whatley, White, Hitchins, Hall G W, J Sperrin, Broadis, Gibbons, Duncan, Ludford.

Millwall (away) won 3-1 (Gibbons 2, Broadis)
Hooper; Ward, Whatley, White, Hitchins, Hall G W, J Sperrin, Broadis, Gibbons, Duncan, Ludford.
Match played at White Hart Lane.

Millwall (home) won 4-0 (Ward, Broadis, Ludford 2)
Hooper; Ward, Whatley, White, Hitchins, Hall GW, J Sperrin, Broadis, Gibbons, Duncan, Ludford.

West Ham United (home) lost 2-1 (Broadis)
Hooper; Wallis, Ward, Hall G W, Hitchins, Bennett L, J Sperrin, Broadis, Gibbons, Skinner, Ludford.

West Ham United (away) lost 3-2 (Gibbons, Hall)
Hooper; Ward, Buckingham, White, Hitchins, Hall G W, J Sperrin, Broadis, Gibbons, Duncan, Ludford.

Reading (home) drew 2-2 (Wallace, Duncan)
Hooper; Ward, Whatley, White, Buckingham, Hall G W, Wallace, Duncan, Gibbons, W Sperrin, Ludford.

Reading (away) drew 2-2 (Duncan, Ludford)
Hooper; Ward, Whatley, White, Hitchins, Buckingham, W Sperrin, Hall G W, Gibbons, Duncan, Ludford.

Arsenal (home) drew 3-3 (Bennett K, Ward, Gibbons)
Hooper; Ward, Howe, White, Hitchins, Hall G W, W Sperrin, Bennett K, Gibbons, Duncan, Ludford.

Arsenal (away) won 3-0 (Duncan 2, Gibbons)
Hooper; Ward, Whatley, White, Hitchins, Hall G W, W Sperrin, Broadis, Gibbons, Duncan, Ludford.
(*NB both Arsenal games played at White Hart Lane*)

Brentford (semi-final home) lost 2-0
Hooper; Ward, Whatley, White, Hitchins, Hall G W, W Sperrin, Broadis, Gibbons, Duncan, Ludford.

Appearances: Bennett K 1, Bennett L 1, I A Broadis 8, Buckingham 3, Duncan 10, A H Gibbons 11, Hall G W 11, Hitchins 10, Hooper 11, Howe 1, Ludford 11, O'Callaghan (Fulham) 1, Skinner 1, J Sperrin 5, W Sperrin 5, J Wallace 1, Wallis 1, Ward 11, Whatley 8, R White 10.

Goals: (32) Gibbons 11, Broadis 5, Duncan 5, Ludford 5, Hall 2, Ward 2, Bennett K 1, Wallace 1.

LONDON LEAGUE 1941-42

Watford (home) won 5-0 (Ludford 3, Gibbons 2)
Hooper; Tickridge, Ward, White, Hitchins, Burgess, W Sperrin, Broadis, Gibbons, Hall G W, Ludford.

Aldershot (away) lost 3-2 (Gibbons 2)
Hooper; Tickridge, Ward, White, Hitchins, Hall G W, W Sperrin, Broadis, Gbbons, Duncan, Ludford.

Millwall (home) won 3-0 (Bennett L, Gibbons, Ludford)
Hooper, Tickridge, Ward, Howe, Hitchins, Hall G W, W Sperrin, Bennett L, Gibbons, Broadis, Ludford.

Arsenal (away) lost 4-0
Hooper; Tickridge, Ward, White, Hitchins, Burgess, W Sperrin, Broadis, Gibbons, Hall G W, Ludford.

Queen's Park Rangers (home) won 3-1 (Ludford 2, Noble)
Hooper; Ward, Tickridge, White, Hitchins, Hall G W, Ludford, Broadis, Woodward, Duncan, Noble.

Reading (away) drew 1-1 (Gibbons)
Hooper; Ward, Tickridge, White, Hitchins, Hall G W, Ludford, Broadis, Gibbons, Duncan, Noble.

Brighton & Hove Albion (home) lst 2-1 (Broadis)
Hooper; Ward, Tickridge, White, Hitchins, Hall G W, R Sainsbury, Broadis, Ludford, Duncan, Noble.

Brentford (away) won 4-1 (Duncan 2, Noble, Ludford)
Hooper; Ward, Tickridge, White, Hall G W, Howe, Ludford, Broadis, Gibbons, Duncan, Noble.

Crystal Palace (home) drew 1-1 (Ludford)
Hooper; Ward, Tickridge, White, Hall G W, Howe, Ludford, Broadis, Gibbons, Duncan, Noble.

Fulham (away) drew 2-2 (Gibbons, Noble)
J Bennett; Ward, Tickridge, White, Hall G W, Whately, Ludford, Broadis, Gibbons, Duncan, Noble.

Clapton Orient (home) won 2-0 (Gibbons, Broadis)
Ditchburn; Ward, Tickridge, White, Hitchins, Whately, Broadis, Hall G W, Gibbons, Duncan, Ludford.

Portsmouth (away) won 2-1 (Ludford, Broadis)
Ditchburn; Ward, Tickridge, White, Hitchins, Hall G W, Ludford, Broadis, Gibbons, Duncan, Williams.

Chelsea (away) drew 1-1 (Duncan)
Ditchburn; Ward, Tickridge, Hall G W, Hitchins, Whately, Cox, Broadis, Gibbons, Duncan, Williams.

Charlton Athletic (away) lost 2-1 (Ludford)
J Bennett; Ward, Tickridge, White, Hitchins, Whately, J Sperrin, Broadis, Ludford, Hall G W, Duncan.

West Ham United (home) drew 1-1 (Broadis)
Ditchburn; Ward, Tickridge, White, Hitchins, Hall G W, W Sperrin, Broadis, Gibbons, Duncan, Williams.

Watford (away) won 2-1 (Hall G W, White)
J Bennett; Ward, Tickridge, White, Hitchins, Hall G W, Ludford, Broadis, Gibbons, Duncan, Gilberg.

Aldershot (home) drew 1-1 (White)
Hooper; Ward, Tickridge, White, Hitchins, Hall G W, Trailor, Broadis, Gibbons, Duncan, Gilberg.

Millwall (away) won 2-1 (Broadis 2)
Ditchburn; Ward, Tickridge, White, Hitchins, Hall G W, W Sperrin, Broadis, Gibbons, Duncan, Ludford.

Arsenal (home) lost 2-1 (Ludford)
Ditchburn; Ward, Tickridge, White, Hall G W, Whately, W Sperrin, Broadis, Gibbons, Duncan, Ludford.

Queen's Park Rangers (away) lost 1-0
Hooper; Ward, Tickridge, White, Hitchins, Hall G W, Ludford, Broadis, Joliffe, Duncan, Gibbons.

Reading (home) won 2-1 (Broadis, Burgess)
Ditchburn; Ward, Tickridge, White, Hitchins, Hall G W,. Sibley, Broadis, Burgess, Duncan, Pearson.

Brighton & Hove Albion (away) lost 5-2 (Sibley, Burgess)
Hooper; Ward, Tickridge, White, Hitchins, Hall G W, Sibley, Broadis, Burgess, Duncan, Pearson.

Crystal Palace (away) drew 2-2 (Ludford, Gibbons)
Hooper; Ward, Tickridge, Burgess, Hitchins, Hall G W, Sibley, Mannion, Gibbons, Duncan, Ludford.

Clapton Orient (away) won 3-2 (Gibbons 3)
Ditchburn; Ward, Tickridge, White, Hitchins, Hall G W, Cox, Mannion, Gibbons, Broadis, Ludford.

Portsmouth (home) drew 1-1 (Gibbons)
Ditchburn; Ward, Tickridge, White, Hitchins, Hall G W, W Sperrin, Broadis, Gibbons, Duncan, Ludford.

Chelsea (home) won 2-0 (Ludford 2)
Hooper; Ward, Tickridge, White, Hitchins, Hall G W, McCormick, Mannion, Ludford, Broadis, Duncan.

Charlton Athletic (home) won 2-0 (Gibbons, Revell)
Hooper; Ward, Tickridge, Hall G W, Hitchins, W Sainsbury, Ludford, Mannion, Gibbons, Broadis, Revell.

West Ham United (away) won 3-2 (Broadis 2, Gibbons)
Ditchburn; Ward, Tickridge, White, Hitchins, W Sainsbury, J Sperrin, Broadis, Gibbons, Duncan, Ludford.

Brentford (home) won 2-1 (Howe, Broadis)
Hooper; Ward, Tickridge, Hall G W, Hitchins, Buckingham, Howe, Broadis, Edwards, Duncan, Ludford.

Fulham (home) won 7-1 (Gibbons 2, Stevens 2, Ludford 2, Broadis)
Ditchburn; Ward, Tickridge, Hall G W, Hitchins, Fitzgerald, Finch, Broadis, Gibbons, Stevens, Ludford.

LONDON CUP 1941-42

Reading (away) won 2-1 (Howe, Ward (pen))
Ditchburn; Ward, Tickridge, White, Hitchins, Hall G W, W Sperrin, Broadis, Gibbons, Howe, Duncan.

Watford (home) won 5-2 (Gibbons 2, Howe, Broadis, Ludford)
Hooper; Ward, Tickridge, Hall G W, Hitchins, Buckingham, Howe, Broadis, Gibbons, Duncan, Ludford.

Reading (home) won 2-1 (Duncan, Ludford)
Ditchburn; Ward, Tickridge, White, Hitchins, Hall G W, Howe, Broadis, Gibbons, Duncan, Ludford.

Watford (away) drew 0-0
Ditchburn; Ward, Tickridge, White, Hall G W, Buckingham, McFarlane, Broadis, Ludford, Duncan, Howe.

Charlton Athletic (home) lost 3-0
Ditchburn; Ward, Tickridge, White, Hitchins, Hall G W, Howe, Kiernan, Gibbons, Broadis, Ludford.

Charlton Athletic (away) lost 4-0
Hooper; Ward, Tickridge, Howe, Hitchins, Burgess, McCormick, Kiernan. Gibbons, Broadis, Edwards.

Appearances: J Bennett (Enfield) 3, Bennett L 1, I A Broadis 35, Buckingham 3, Burgess 6, Cox 2, Ditchburn 15, Duncan 28, R Edwards (Alloa) 2, Finch (Fulham) 1, Fitzgerald (QPR) 1, A H Gibbons 28, H Gilberg 2, Hall G W 34, Hitchins 31, Hooper 18, Howe 10, Joliffe (HAC) 1, Kiernan (Albion R) 2, Ludford 29, Mannion (Middlesbrough) 4, McCormick 2, McFarlane (Nottm F) 1, Noble (Clyde) 6, Pearson (Newcastle) 2, Revell (Charlton) 1, R Sainsbury 1, W Sainsbury 2, Sibley (Southend) 3, J Sperrin 2, W Sperrin 9, Stevens 1, S Tickridge 36, Trailor 1, Ward 36, Whately 5, R White 28, Williams (Bristol C) 3, H Woodward (Finchley) 1.

Goals: (70) Gibbons 19, Ludford 18, Broadis 12, Duncan 4, Howe 3, Noble 3, Burgess 2, Stevens 2, White 2, Bennett L 1, Hall 1, Revell 1, Sibley 1, Ward 1.

WATFORD

LONDON LEAGUE 1941-42

Tottenham Hotspur (away) lost 5-0
W Jones; Harris, Davidson, Fitzsimmons, Galley, Woodward, Jones T, Barnett, Learmouth, McIntosh, R Williams.

Portsmouth (home) lost 5-1 (Galley)
W Jones; Harris, Davidson, Fitzsimmons, Woodward, Cringan, Jones T, Barnett, Galley, McIntosh, Salltall.

Chelsea (home) lost 3-1 (Biggs)
Boulton; Woodward, Davidson, Fitzsimmons, Galley, R Williams, Jones T, Barnett, Biggs, McIntosh, Bonass.

Charlton Athletic (away) lost 5-1 (Biggs)
Boulton; Harris, Woodward, Jones T, Cringan, R Williams, Barnett, Lewis H, Biggs, McIntosh, Bonass.

West Ham United (home) lost 8-0
Boulton; Jones T, Lewis J, Woodward, Galley, R Williams, Barnett, T Robinson, Biggs, Lewis H, Drinkwater.

Clapton Orient (home) drew 2-2 (Galley, Waller)
Boulton; Harris, Wainwright, Briggs, Galley, R Williams, Jones T, Lewis H, Waller, McIntosh, Drinkwater.

Aldershot (away) lost 8-1 (Briggs)
Boulton; Jones S, Lewis J, Briggs, Fitzsimmons, R Williams, Jones T, Lewis H, Waller, McIntosh, Drinkwater,.

Millwall (away) lost 4-2 (Westcott 2)
Boulton; Harris, Davidson, Briggs, Hughes, R Williams, Jones T, Morris, Westcott, McIntosh, Drinkwater.

Arsenal (home) won 3-1 (Jones T, Morris, Killhourhy)
Boulton; Harris, R Williams, Briggs, Hughes, Cringan, Jones T, Morris, Walters, Killhourhy, Drinkwater.

Queen's Park Rangers (away) won 5-1 (Westcott 5)
Boulton; Harris, R Williams, Briggs, Woodward, Cringan, Jones T, Morris, Westcott, Killhourhy, Drinkwater.

Reading (home) drew 0-0
Boulton; Jones T, R Williams, Briggs, Woodward, Cringan, Davies W, Morris, Killhourhy, Lewis H, Drinkwater.

Brighton & Hove Albion (away) drew 2-2 (Broome, T Robinson)
Boulton; Jones T, Blandford, Briggs, Woodward, Cringan, Broome, Morris, T Robinson, Killhourhy, Evans.

Brentford (home) lost 6-1 (Killhourhy)
Boulton; Jones T, Lewis G, Briggs, Woodward, Cringan, Morris, Armstrong, Learmouth, Killhourhy, Burley.

Crystal Palace (away) lost 6-1 (Lewis G)
W Jones; Jones T, Woodward, Reece, Robinson T W, Cringan, Lewis H, Barnett, Lewis G, Killhourhy, Findlay.

Fulham (home) lost 5-3 (Cringan, Lewis H, Barnett)
Boulton; Jones T, Woodward, Cowie, Robinson T W, Cringan, Lewis H, Barnett, Walters, Morris, Ward.

Tottenham Hotspur (home) lost 2-1 (Egan)
Jepson; Harris, Woodward, Jones T, Robinson T W, Cringan, Croom, Barnett, Delaney, Egan, Wipfler.

Portsmouth (away) lost 7-1 (Griffiths (pen))
W Jones; Sykes, Woodward, Jones T, Robinson T W, Cringan, Mansell, Barnett, R Williams, Griffiths, Brown J.

Chelsea (away) drew 2-2 (Morris, Brown)
Davison; Harris, Jobling, Jones T, Robinson T W, Bearryman, Jones E, Morris, Egan, Griffiths, Brown J.

Charlton Athletic (home) lost 2-1 (Morris)
Davison; Jones T, Jobling, Weightman, Robinson T W, R Williams, Jones E, Morris, Egan, Griffiths, Findlay.

West Ham United (away) lost 4-1 (Jones E)
Davison; Cowie, Jobling, Jones T, R Williams, Weightman, Jones E, Morris, Griffiths, Davies W, Brown J.

Clapton Orient (away) lost 2-0
Davison; Harris, Jobling, Cowie, Robinson T W, Weightman, Jones E, Jones T, Henson, Galley, Halford.

Arsenal (away) lost 11-0
Davison; Jobling, R Williams, Cowie, Sliman, Cringan, Woodgate, Jones T, Walker, Hall, Brown.J.

Reading (away) lost 5-1 (Killhourhy)
Jepson; Robinson T W, Jobling, Jones T, Galley, Cringan, Wilson, Morris, Hutton, Killhourhy, Jones E.

Brighton & Hove Albion (home) won 7-1 (Jones T 2, Killhourhy 2, Kurz, Lewis G, Jones E)
Jepson; Jobling, R Williams, Smith, Robinson T W, Cringan, Jones T, Kurz, Lewis G, Killhourhy, Jones E.

Brentford (away) lost 5-3 (Hutton 2, Lancelotte)
Jepson; Gregory, Harris, Jones T, Lane, Cringan, Morris, Lancelotte, Hutton, Killhourhy, Barrs.

Crystal Palace (home) won 2-1 (Lewis G, Halford)
Jepson; Harris, Jobling, Evans, Robinson T W, R Williams, Jones T, Morris, Lewis G, Killhourhy, Halford.

Fulham (away) won 3-1 (Jones T, Hutton, Wipfler)
Jepson; Harris, Jobling, Jones T, Robinson T W, Dugnolle, Jones E, Kurz, Hutton, Morris, Wipfler.

Aldershot (home) lost 5-1 (Keeton og))
N Watson-Smith; Harris, Jobling, Dugnolle, Robinson T W, Hamilton, Jones E, Kurz, Walters, Killhourhy, Bacon.

Queen's Park Rangers (home) lost 5-0
N Watson-Smith; Harris, Jobling, Jones T, Robinson T W, Holliday, Jones E, Kurz, Walters, Killhourhy, Brown.J

Millwall (home) won 1-0 (Jones E (pen))
Jepson; G Cooke, Jobling, Whittaker, Hitchins, R Williams, Jones T, Dougall, Kurz, Hobbis, Jones E.

LONDON CUP 1941-42

Charlton Ahtletic (home) lost 4-1 (Kurz)
Jepson; Harris, R Williams, Jones T, Robinson T W, Dugnolle, Jones E, Miller, Kurz, Killhourhy, Halford.

Tottenham Hotspur (away) lost 5-2 (Westcott, Killhourhy)
Jepson; Harris, Evans, Jones T, Robinson T W, Galley, Jones E, Kurz, Westcott, Killhourhy, Halford.

Charlton Athletic (away) won 1-0 (Dougall)
Jepson; Harris, Davidson, Jones T, Robinson T W, Dugnolle, Jones E, Dougall, Kurz, Killhourhy, Brown.J

Tottenham Hotspur (home) drew 0-0
N Watson-Smith; Jobling, Davidson, Jones T, Robinson T W, R Wiliams, Jones E, Dougall, Kurz, Killhourhy, Brown J.

Reading (home) won 6-0 (Kurz 4, Killhourhy, Brown)
Jepson; Harris, Jobling, Jones T, Robinson T W, Dugnolle, Jones E, Dougall, Kurz, Killhourhy, Brown J.

Reading (away) lost 3-0
Sgt Brown; Harris, R Williams, Jones T, Jobling, Dugnolle, Brown J, Dougall, Kurz, Cockburn, Durman.

Appearances: Armstrong (Bristol C) 1, Bacon (Chelsea) 1, Barnett 9, Barrs (Southampton) 1, Bearryman (Chelsea) 1, Biggs (Aberdeen) 3, Blandford (Gainsborough) 1, Bonass (QPR) 2, Boulton (Derby) 12, Briggs (Wrexham) 8, Broome (Villa) 1, Brown J (Frickley CW) 9, S Brown (Army) 1, Burley (QPR) 1, Cockburn* 1, G Cooke (Barking) 1, Cowie (Aberdeen) 4, Cringan (Cardiff) 15, Croom (Leeds) 1, Davidson (Bradford PA) 6, Davies 2, Davison (Blackburn) 5, Delaney (Army) 1, Dougall (Burnley) 5, Drinkwater (Villa) 7, Dugnolle (Plymouth) 6, Durman* 1, Egan (Aldershot) 3, Evans 3, Findlay (ex-Watford) 2, Fitzsimmons (QoS) 4, Galley (Wolves) 8, Gregory F (C Palace) 1, Griffiths (Tranmere) 4, Halford (Oldham) 4, Hall A (Spurs) 1, Hamilton (St Bernards) 1, Harris 20, Henson (Sheff U) 1, Hitchins (Spurs) 1, Hobbis (Charlton) 1, Holliday (Brentford) 1, Hughes (N Brighton) 2, Hutton (Halifax) 3, Jepson (Port Vale) 11, Jobling (Charlton) 15, Jones E (WBA) 15, Jones S (Arsenal) 1, Jones T 35, W Jones (St Albans) 4, Killhourhy (Doncaster) 17, Kurz (Grimsby) 11, Lancelotte (Charlton) 1, Lane (ex-Orient) 1, Learmouth (Partick) 2, Lewis G 4, Lewis H 7, Lewis J 2, McIntosh (Wolves) 7, Mansell (Army) 1, Miller (Northampton) 1, Morris (RAF) 14, Reece (C Palace) 1, T Robinson (Wisbech) 2, Robinson T W (Barnsley) 18, Salltall (Bristol C) 1, Sliman (Chelmsford) 1, Smith (Charlton) 1, Sykes (Millwall) 1, Wainwright (Man U) 1, Walker* 1, Waller (Arsenal) 2, Walters (Dartford) 4, Ward (Sheff W) 1, N Watson-Smith (Yorkshire Amat) 3, Weightman (Notts Co) 3, Westcott (Wolves) 3, Whittaker (Charlton) 1, R Williams 20, Wilson* 1, Wipfler (Frickley CW) 2, Woodgate (West Ham) 1, Woodward 13.

Goals: (57) Westcott 8, Killhourhy 7, Kurz 6, Jones T 4, Hutton 3, Jones E 3, Lewis G 3, Morris 3, Biggs 2, Brown J 2, Galley 2, Barnett 1, Briggs 1, Broome 1, Cringan 1, Dougall 1, Egan 1, Griffiths 1, Halford 1, Lewis H 1, Lancelotte 1, T Robinson 1, Waller 1, Wipfler 1, own goal 1.

WEST HAM UNITED

LONDON CUP 1940-41

Millwall (away) won 2-1 (Foreman, Goulden)
Medhurst; Bicknell, Chalkley, Small, Barrett, Fenton, Foxall, Macaulay, Foreman, Goulden, Hobbis.

Millwall (home) won 2-1 (Foreman, Hobbis)
Gregory; Bicknell, Chalkley, Small, Barrett, Fenton, Foxall, Macaulay, Foreman, Goulden, Hobbis.

Arsenal (home) lost 3-1 (Bicknell)
Gregory; Bicknell, Chalkley, Small, Fenton, Savage, Foxall, Macaulay, Foreman, Goulden, Hobbis.

Tottenham Hotspur (away) won 2-1 (Small, Fenton)
Medhurst; Bicknell, Savage, Small, Barrett, Green, Foxall, Fenton, Foreman, Goulden, Hobbis.

Tottenham Hotspur (home) won 3-2 (Foreman, Small, Foxall)
Gregory; Bicknell, Savage, Barrett, Walker R, Green, Foxall, Small, Foreman, Fenton, Hobbis.

Reading (home) drew 1-1 (Hobbis)
Medhurst; Bicknell, Banner, Small, Corbett N, Lewis, Foxall, Macaulay, Foreman, Goulden, Hobbis.

Reading (away) lost 4-1 (Wood)
Medhurst; Bicknell, Chalkley, Small, Walker R, Corbett N, Foxall, Wood, Foreman, Goulden, Hobbis.

Clapton Orient (home) won 8-1 (Foreman 2, Small 2, Foxall, Corbett, Goulden, Chalkley)
Gregory; Bicknell, Chalkley, Waller, Barrett, Corbett N, Nieuwenhuys, Small, Foreman, Goulden, Foxall.

Clapton Orient (away) won 3-2 (Foreman 2, Small)
Medhurst; Bicknell, Chalkley, Collier, Waller, Lewis, Foxall, Small, Foreman, Goulden, Hobbis.

Arsenal (away) lost 3-0
Gregory; Bicknell, Chalkley, Corbett N, Barrett, Lewis, Foxall, Chapman, Foreman, Small, Hobbis.

Appearances: Banner 1, Barrett 6, Bicknell 10, Chalkley 7, E Chapman 1, A Collier 1, Corbett N 4, Fenton 5, Foreman 10, Foxall 10, Goulden 8, Green (Charlton) 2, Gregory 5, Hobbis (Charlton) 9, W Lewis 3, Macaulay 4, Medhurst 5, Nieuwenhuys (Liverpool) 1, Savage (Wrexham) 3, Small 10, Walker R 2, Waller (Arsenal) 2, Wood 1.

Goals: (23) Foreman 7, Small 5, Foxall 2, Goulden 2, Hobbis 2, Bicknell 1, Chalkley 1, Corbett 1, Fenton 1, Wood 1.

LONDON LEAGUE 1941-42

Portsmouth (home) lost 3-1 (Foxall)
Medhurst; Bicknell, Chalkley, Fenton, Walker R, Corbett N, Small, Macaulay, Foreman, Goulden, Foxall.

Chelsea (away) won 8-4 (Foreman 3, Foxall 2, Small, Fenton, Goulden)
Gregory; Bicknell, Chalkley, Fenton, Barrett, Lewis, Nieuwenhuys, Small, Foreman, Goulden, Foxall.

Charlton Athletic (away) drew 1-1 (Foreman)
Medhurst; Bicknell, Chalkley, Corbett N, Walker R, Fenton, Nieuwenhuys, Small, Foreman, Goulden, Foxall.

Clapton Orient (home) won 3-1 (Macaulay, Foreman, Foxall)
Gregory; Bicknell, Chalkley, Small, Barrett, Fenton, Nieuwenhuys, Macaulay, Foreman, Goulden, Foxall.

Watford (away) won 8-0 (Foreman 3, Foxall 2, Nieuwenhuys 2, Small)
Medhurst; Bicknell, Chalkley, Corbett N, Walker R, Fenton, Nieuwenhuys, Small, Foreman, Goulden, Foxall.

Aldershot (home) won 3-0 (Foreman 2, Barrett)
Gregory; Bicknell, Chalkley, Fenton, Barrett, Attwell, Small, Macaulay, Foreman, Goulden, Foxall.

Millwall (home) won 4-2 (Foreman 2, Nieuwenhuys, Bicknell)
Medhurst; Bicknell, Chalkley, Fenton, Walker R, Attwell, Nieuwenhuys, Small, Foreman, Goulden, Foxall.

Arsenal (away) lost 4-1 (Foreman)
Gregory; Bicknell, Chalkley, Fenton, Walker R, Corbett N, Nieuwenhuys, Small, Foreman, Goulden, Foxall.

Queen's Park Rangers (home) won 2-0 (Macaulay, Foreman)
Medhurst; Bicknell, Chalkley, Fenton, Barrett, Corbett N, Small, Macaulay, Foreman, Goullden, Foxall.

Reading (away) lost 3-2 (Bicknell, Macaulay)
Gregory; Bicknell, Chalkley, Fenton, Walker R, Attwell, Small, Macaulay, Foreman, Goulden, Foxall.

Brighton & Hove Albion (home) won 4-0 (Foreman 2, Goulden 2)
Taylor; Corbett N, Banner, Fenton, Barrett, Small, Nieuwenhuys, Macaulay, Foreman, Goulden, Foxall.

Brentford (away) won 5-0 (Foxall 2, Small 2, Goulden)
Gregory; Bicknell, Chalkley, Fenton, Walker R, Attwell, Small, Macaulay, Foreman, Goulden, Foxall.
Crystal Palace (home) lost 5-0
Barrett; Bicknell, Chalkley, Lewis, Fenton, Attwell, Nieuwenhuys, Small, Foreman, Goulden, Foxall.

Fulham (away) won 3-1 (Small 2, Goulden)
Medhurst; Bicknell, Chalkley, Fenton, Barrett, Corbett N, Small, Wood, Foreman, Goulden, Foxall.

Tottenham Hotspur (away) drew 1-1 (Foxall)
Gregory; Walker C, Whately, Fenton, Walker R, Corbett N, Small, Macaulay, Foreman, Goulden, Foxall.

Portsmouth (away) lost 1-0
Gregory; Bicknell, Jobling, Waller, Barrett, Lewis, Chapman, Fenton, Foreman, Goulden, Foxall.

Chelsea (home) won 5-0 (Foreman, Fenton, Goulden, Foxall, Macaulay)
Medhurst; Bicknell, Banner, Fenton, Walker R, Corbett N, Small, Macaulay, Foreman, Goulden, Foxall.

Charlton Athletic (home) drew 2-2 (Foxall, Bicknell)
Gregory; Bicknell, Chalkley, Fenton, Corbett N, Attwell, Wood, Macaulay, Foreman, Goulden, Foxall.

Clapton Orient (away) lost 3-1 (Chapman)
Rickett; Bicknell, Banner, Chalkley, Barrett, Corbett N, Chapman, Small, Foreman, Fenton, Foxall.

Watford (home) won 4-1 (Wood 3, Foxall)
Medhurst; Corbett N, Lewis, Fenton, Sliman, Attwell, Small, Wood, Foreman, Goulden, Foxall.

Aldershot (away) won 5-1 (Chapman 3, Foreman, Quickenden)
Gregory; Bicknell, Lewis, Tann, Fenton, Macaulay, Quickenden, Chapman, Foreman, Goulden, Foxall.

Millwall (away) won 3-1 (Chapman, Foxall, Small)
Medhurst; Bicknell, Lewis, Fenton, Walker R, Macaulay, Small, Chapman, Foreman, Goulden, Foxall.

Arsenal (home) won 3-0 (Foreman 2, Goulden)
Gregory; Bicknell, Walker C, Fenton, Barrett, Macaulay, Small, Chapman, Foreman, Goulden, Foxall.

Queen's Park Rangers (away) lost 2-1 (Small)
Medhurst; Bicknell, Banner, Corbett N, Fenton, Lewis, Small, Chapman, Foreman, Goulden, Foxall.

Brighton & Hove Albion (away) won 3-1 (Foreman, Small, Goulden)
Medhurst; Banner, Chalkley, Corbett N, Fenton, Lewis, Small, Dunn, Foreman, Goulden, Foxall.

Brentford (home) won 2-1 (Small, Goulden)
Gregory; Bicknell, Forde, Pryde, Fenton, Lewis, Small, Dunn, Foreman, Goulden, Foxall.

Crystal Palace (away) drew 1-1 (Small)
Medhurst; Chalkley, Banner, Bicknell, Walker R, Corbett N, Small, Fenton, Foreman, Goulden, Foxall.

Fulham (home) drew 1-1 (Goulden)
Medhurst; Bicknell, Lewis, Walker R, Fenton, Attwell, Small, Jones, Foreman, Goulden, Foxall.

Tottenham Hotspur (home) lost 3-2 (Fenton, Goulden)
Gregory; Corbett N, Lewis, Attwell, Walker R, Macaulay, Small, Fenton, Foreman, Goulden, Foxall.

Reading (home) won 2-1 (Mahon, Chapman)
Taylor; Chalkley, Banner, Walker R, Macaulay, Lewis, Chapman, Dunn, Foreman, Goulden, Mahon.

LONDON CUP 1941-42

Brighton & Hove Albion (away) won 2-1 (Foxall, Foreman)
Taylor; Bicknell, Chalkley, Lewis, Fenton, Attwell, Small, Wood, Foreman, Goulden, Foxall.

Arsenal (home) lost 4-0
Gregory; Bicknell, Chalkley, Corbett N, Walker R, Fenton, Nieuwenhuys, Small, Foreman, Goulden, Foxall.

Brighton & Hove Albion (home) won 6-2 (Foreman 3, Mahon 2, Fenton)
Rickett; Bicknell, Lewis, Waller, Barrett, Fenton, Mahon, Small, Foreman, Goulden, Gore.

Arsenal (away) won 4-1 (Goulden 2, Small, Fenton)
Gregory; Bicknell, Chalkley, Fenton, Walker R, Corbett N, Nieuwenhuys, Small, Foreman, Goulden, Foxall.

Clapton Orient (home) won 5-3 (Foreman 2, Wood 2, Corbett)
Gregory; Bicknell, Walker C, Corbett N, Fenton, Attwell, Small, Wood, Foreman, Goulden, Mahon.

Clapton Orient (away) won 1-0 (Foreman)
Medhurst; Chalkley, Lewis, Bicknall, Corbett N, Walker C, Mahon, Wood, Foreman, Goulden, Gore.

Appearances: Attwell 11, Banner 7, Barrett 11, Bicknell 30, Chalkley 22, E Chapman 7, Corbett N 20, Dunn 3, Fenton 34, Forde 1, Foreman 36, Foxall 32, Gore 2, Goulden 35, Gregory 16, Jobling (Charlton) 1, Jones L (Arsenal) 1, W Lewis 15, Macaulay 15, Mahon (Huddersfield) 4, Medhurst 14, Nieuwenhuys (Liverpool) 10, Pryde (Arsenal) 1, R Quickenden 1, Rickett (Chelmsford) 2, Sliman (Chelmsford) 1, Small 31, Tann (Charlton) 1, Taylor 3, Walker C 4, Walker R 16, Waller (Arsenal) 2, Whately (Spurs) 1, Wood 6.

Goals: (99) Foreman 28, Foxall 14, Goulden 13, Small 12, Chapman 6, Fenton 5, Wood 5, Macaulay 4, Bicknell 3, Mahon 3, Nieuwenhuys 3, Barrett 1, Corbett 1, Quickenden 1.

FINAL TABLES

LONDON LEAGUE 1941-42

	P	*W*	*D*	*L*	*F*	*A*	*Pts*
Arsenal	30	23	2	5	108	43	48
Portsmouth	30	20	2	8	105	59	42
West Ham United	30	17	5	8	81	44	39
Aldershot	30	17	5	8	85	56	39
Tottenham Hotspur	30	15	8	7	61	41	38
Crystal Palace	30	14	6	10	70	53	34
Reading	30	13	8	9	76	58	34
Charlton Athletic	30	14	5	11	72	64	33
Brentford	30	14	2	14	80	76	30
Queen's Park Rangers	30	11	3	16	52	59	25
Fulham	30	10	4	16	79	99	24
Brighton & Hove Albion	30	9	4	17	71	108	22
Chelsea	30	8	4	18	56	88	20
Millwall	30	7	5	18	53	82	19
Clapton Orient	30	5	7	18	42	94	17
Watford	30	6	4	20	47	114	16

LONDON CUP 1940-41

Group A

	P	*W*	*D*	*L*	*F*	*A*	*Pts*
Brentford	10	4	5	1	25	20	13
Crystal Palace	10	4	4	2	25	18	12
Queen's Park Rangers	10	5	1	4	26	26	11
Aldershot	10	4	2	4	21	24	10
Fulham	10	4	0	6	32	34	8
Chelsea	10	2	2	6	19	26	6

Group B

	P	*W*	*D*	*L*	*F*	*A*	*Pts*
Reading	10	6	4	0	29	8	16
Tottenham Hotspur	10	5	3	2	32	14	13
West Ham United	10	6	1	3	23	19	13
Arsenal	10	5	2	3	38	18	12
Millwall	10	2	1	7	13	26	5
Clapton Orient	10	0	1	9	9	59	1

LONDON CUP 1941-42

Group 1

	P	W	D	L	F	A	Pts
Arsenal	6	5	0	1	19	7	10
West Ham United	6	5	0	1	18	11	10
Clapton Orient	6	1	0	5	10	19	2
Brighton & Hove Albion	6	1	0	5	11	21	2

Group 2

	P	W	D	L	F	A	Pts
Brentford	6	4	2	0	17	9	10
Millwall	6	2	3	1	15	12	7
Queen's Park Rangers	6	2	1	3	8	7	5
Aldershot	6	1	0	5	8	20	2

Group 3

	P	W	D	L	F	A	Pts
Charlton Athletic	6	4	1	1	17	6	9
Tottenham Hotspur	6	3	1	2	9	11	7
Watford	6	2	1	3	10	12	5
Reading	6	1	1	4	9	16	3

Group 4

	P	W	D	L	F	A	Pts
Portsmouth	6	4	1	1	16	4	9
Fulham	6	4	1	1	14	16	9
Chelsea	6	1	3	2	8	8	5
Crystal Palace	6	0	1	5	8	18	1

LONDON LEAGUE 1941-42: RESULTS

	Aldershot	Arsenal	Brentford	Brighton	Charlton	Chelsea	C Orient	C Palace	Fulham	Millwall	Portsmouth	QPR	Reading	Tottenham	Watford	West Ham
Aldershot	X	1-0	6-3	5-1	1-0	2-3	1-1	1-2	4-3	5-2	3-2	4-1	0-0	3-2	8-1	1-5
Arsenal	3-2	X	1-3	4-2	3-2	3-0	5-2	7-2	2-0	10-0	6-1	4-1	3-1	4-0	11-0	4-1
Brentford	5-1	4-1	X	4-2	2-1	3-1	5-2	1-2	2-3	4-3	2-5	4-3	3-2	1-4	5-3	0-5
Brighton	1-5	2-3	2-2	X	3-5	8-2	4-1	2-2	3-7	5-0	2-1	2-5	1-5	5-2	2-2	1-3
Charlton	1-5	1-3	3-2	8-2	X	2-1	4-0	3-1	3-3	1-2	2-5	3-1	2-3	2-1	5-1	1-1
Chelsea	4-0	1-5	1-1	1-3	2-4	X	1-3	1-0	1-5	3-3	3-4	3-1	0-5	1-1	2-2	4-8
C Orient	0-5	1-3	1-3	3-3	1-1	0-3	X	4-0	2-1	3-3	0-4	0-0	3-8	2-3	2-0	3-1
C Palace	1-2	3-3	2-0	10-1	4-0	3-2	2-0	X	3-1	2-0	3-1	2-1	1-1	2-2	6-1	1-1
Fulham	2-6	2-5	4-3	2-3	4-7	1-4	5-1	4-3	X	4-3	2-7	0-3	2-2	2-2	1-3	1-3
Millwall	3-1	2-2	4-2	2-0	0-1	6-3	2-2	1-0	2-4	X	1-3	1-2	1-1	1-2	4-2	1-3
Portsmouth	2-2	1-5	2-1	5-3	7-2	2-3	16-1	3-1	5-3	3-2	X	3-1	1-0	1-2	7-1	1-0
QPR	0-2	0-1	3-4	3-0	0-0	2-1	2-1	1-3	2-5	4-1	0-2	X	4-0	1-0	1-5	2-1
Reading	3-3	1-4	4-3	4-5	1-4	3-2	2-0	6-2	4-1	2-1	5-2	2-2	X	1-1	5-1	3-2
Tottenham	1-1	1-2	2-1	1-2	2-0	2-0	2-0	1-1	7-1	3-0	1-1	3-1	2-1	X	5-0	1-1
Watford	1-5	3-1	1-6	7-1	1-2	1-3	2-2	2-1	3-5	1-0	1-5	0-5	0-0	1-2	X	0-8
West Ham	3-0	3-0	2-1	4-0	2-2	5-0	3-1	0-5	1-1	4-2	1-3	2-0	2-1	2-3	4-1	X

LONDON LEAGUE 1941-42: ATTENDANCES

	Aldershot	Arsenal	Brentford	Brighton	Charlton	Chelsea	C Orient	C Palace	Fulham	Millwall	Portsmouth	QPR	Reading	Tottenham	Watford	West Ham
Aldershot	X	8700	3000	3000	5316	6000	2500	2000	3000	3000	4715	4000	3752	5000	3000	3500
Arsenal	8884	X	9739	6206	3958	7747	7036	6207	10578	7520	10160	7377	8198	17446	4701	13419
Brentford	4410	12000	X	5000	6320	6000	3420	4700	3000	3960	3820	3500	6100	6000	3110	5000
Brighton	4500	10000	5000	X	4800	2500	4000	4000	2500	3000	4250	3000	2400	2000	4000	3000
Charlton	3011	13910	3959	944	X	6793	3565	2760	3091	5797	4901	2305	3288	4210	3663	7673
Chelsea	6000	12260	3135	3000	3500	X	2718	3000	3255	3442	3258	1829	2945	6718	4132	6427
C Orient	1500	6000	3500	2000	1000	2000	X	2000	2000	1200	2403	2000	2000	4500	1200	3000
C Palace	5700	10024	6000	4771	5300	5583	3400	X	5000	4764	5493	4500	3550	5332	4000	7790
Fulham	3500	10473	6000	2500	3091	4994	1921	3000	X	1000	4404	3771	6019	6000	2462	4468
Millwall	2000	15000	2000	1000	6742	5500	2000	5100	5000	X	3507	1000	3700	6000	2500	4000
Portsmouth	6328	15785	5806	4190	4336	6469	5010	4515	6324	6217	X	4251	5441	6044	4633	6319
QPR	3086	8932	8000	3000	5500	6000	2000	6900	5500	3500	2935	X	3400	4500	3000	5000
Reading	6000	10000	5159	4041	4000	3128	2809	4000	4667	4200	3888	3177	X	5484	2628	6000
Tottenham	4250	16777	5131	4542	4641	6558	5685	4807	3754	6656	4813	5955	4418	X	5074	8493
Watford	2067	6000	4000	1000	2347	4000	2000	500	1000	1686	3691	1721	4370	3000	X	4000
West Ham	5500	20000	4000	5600	9789	3800	4500	7000	2500	7500	6250	5300	4321	7986	4000	X

SOME OTHER SOCCERDATA TITLES BY JACK ROLLIN

SOCCER IN THE 1930s
Simple Or Sublime?
ISBN 978-1-905891-92-4
Price £18. 248 page illustrated paperback
Soccer in the 1930s has a narrative part, telling the story of 1930s football in the home nations, and a fifty page statistical section. The book is structured around chapters that give details of the careers of the players of the time, a survey of the achievements of all the League clubs around the country, and a chapter of miscellaneous items that lend colour to the events of the time. Football in Scotland, Wales and Ireland is not neglected. Nor is the fledging World Cup, three competitions of which took place in the 1930s, without any UK involvement of course. The book is illustrated with player photographs, team groups and action shots.

THE MEN WHO NEVER WERE
The Football League Season of 1939-40
ISBN: 978-1-905891-11-5
Price £12. 118 page illustrated paperback
1939-40 started on August 26 with a full programme of Football League fixtures, with many newly-signed players in the teams. After the declaration of war on September 2 the official League programme came to an end and the records of the three matches were expunged from the records. Therefore, many of the new players do not appear in a club's official records. The book starts with the story of the 1939 close season and recounts the effects of the outbreak of war on the players and the clubs. With many men enlisted in the servicesand based at Aldershot, the local club enjoyed a succession of star players as guests in their team. Statistical content includes full results, scorers and line-ups for the Football League and War Cup games of 1939-40 with details of all the players that took part. Also included are the results and dates of the many regional competitions that were played that season.

THE FORGOTTEN FA CUP
The Competition Of 1945-46
ISBN: 978-1-899468-86-7
Price £10. 102 page illustrated paperback
1945-46 was a transitional season for football. The end of the war in Europe and the Far East came too late for many professional players to be demobbed from the services, so the formal League programme was not resumed until 1946-47. However, a full programme of FA Cup games took place. The rounds proper featured the only two-legged ties in the history of the competition. Huge attendances watched the games. The books tells the full story of the 1945-46 competition, with player reminiscences and contemporary accounts. Contents also include full results of the qualifying rounds, complete line-ups and scorers for the rounds proper, and a list of all the players that took part. The book also includes all Football League results and dates from the regional competitions that were played in that season.